THE POLITICS OF
PENAL REFORM

KU-207-473

Mick Ryan

LONGMAN
London and New York

LONGMAN GROUP LIMITED
Longman House, Burnt Mill, Harlow
Essex CM20 2JE, England
Associated companies, branches and representatives throughout the world

*Published in the United States of America
by Longman Inc., New York*

First published 1983

BRITISH LIBRARY CATALOGUING IN PUBLICATION DATA
Ryan, Mick
    The politics of penal reform. — (Politics today)
    1. Punishment — Great Britain
    2. Corrections — Great Britain
    I. Title
    364.6'0941   HV9647
    ISBN 0-582-29539-4

LIBRARY OF CONGRESS CATALOGING IN PUBLICATION DATA
Ryan, Mick.
    The politics of penal reform.

    (Politics today)
    Bibliography: p. 142
    Includes index.
    1. Corrections — Government policy — Great Britain —
History — 20th century.   2. Great Britain — Politics and
Government — 1945-   . I. Title. II. Series.
HV9644.R92   1983   365'.7'0941   82-17956
ISBN 0-582-29539-4

Set in 10/11 Linotron 202 Plantin
Printed in Singapore by
Four Strong Printing Co.

CONTENTS

EDITORS' PREFACE

There is a demand among the general public as well as from students for books that deal with the main issues of modern British politics in such a way that the reader can gain a reliable account of how an issue arose, of its institutional context and then, but only then, to have argument about what should be done.

Behind what have become political issues, there are fundamental problems. Many books identify these problems theoretically, but too often ignore the empirical context, and others are so polemical and doctrinaire that their conclusions, however just, are distrusted by shrewd readers. We believe in casting out neither facts nor values, but in relating them closely but distinctly. The test of a good book on political issues should be that a reader will feel that he has a full and reliable account of how the issue arose and what institutions and groups affect and are affected by it, irrespective of what the author thinks should be done. But authors cannot just describe, inevitably they prescribe; so let it be done openly and clearly. Politics is too important for neutrality, but therefore demanding of objectivity. So we ask the authors in this series to organise the books into three parts: the recent history of the matter, the institutional setting, and argument about the future.

We believe that relevant books are wanted, neither wholly committed books nor those that pretend to scientific objectivity. This series continues work that we began with Fontana Books, in their 'Political Issues' series. Some similarities will be obvious, particularly in our injunction to authors to write at the highest possible level of intelligence but to eschew all jargon and technicalities. Students of politics should accept, not worry, that they have a public role.

Bernard Crick and Patrick Seyd

AUTHOR'S PREFACE

To divide the postwar period into three phases I have settled on the years 1959 and 1970. It is important to remember that these dates have been singled out because certain events or publications in those years showed that attitudes towards the penal system were beginning to change. In no way do I wish to suggest that it was in these particular years that the balance was decisively shifted from reform to rehabilitation and then from rehabilitation to justice.

During the last decade or so sociologists have helped to enlarge our understanding of deviant or criminal behaviour, to place it in a wider social and political context. I have tried to explain these critical developments for the general reader in as straightforward a way as possible.

I have compiled a short, select bibliography which points very directly to the sources I have used most. Apart from the obvious academic help this signifies, I would also like to thank Robert Kilroy-Silk MP, Tim Owen (RAP) and Martin Wright (Howard League) for looking through my manuscript and making a number of useful suggestions.

To the editors Bernard Crick and Patrick Seyd my special thanks; their sometimes detailed criticisms were invaluable.

The librarians at Thames Polytechnic were, as always, most helpful, especially Imogen Forster. Ann Holland, Vivien Redman and Josephine Birchenough (in particular) helped to transcribe and type my manuscript. They deserve my special thanks.

This is also an appropriate occasion to express my gratitude to Elizabeth Wardle (née Wilkin) who finally persuaded me to go to university. To Joan Ryan, of course, my warmest thanks for always being prepared to read, discuss and criticize my work. She has made a significant contribution to this book.

Mick Ryan

LIST OF ABBREVIATIONS

ACPS	Advisory Council on the Penal System
ACTO	Advisory Council on the Treatment of Offenders
Howard League	Howard League for Penal Reform
MUFTI	Minimal Use of Force Tactical Intervention
NACRO	National Association for the Care and Resettlement of Offenders
NCCL	National Council for Civil Liberties
PROP	Preservation of the Rights of Prisoners
POA	Prison Officers Association
RAP	Radical Alternatives to Prison

ACKNOWLEDGEMENTS

We are indebted to the following for permission to reproduce copyright material:

Heinemann Educational Books for extracts from *Change, Choice and Conflict* by Hall *et al.*, and *Crime, Criminology and Public Policy* by R. Hood; Macmillan, London and Basingstoke and Holmes & Meier Inc. for extracts from pp. 11 and 52 *Policing the Crisis* (1978) by Stuart Hall *et al.*; the author, J. S. McCarthy for extracts from his letter to *The Times* 19 Nov. 1981; Scottish Academic Press Ltd for an extract from *The Coming Penal Crisis* by Bottoms & Preston; University of Cambridge, Institute of Criminology for extracts from *Penal Policy Making in England*.

INTRODUCTION

In interpretations of the mugging panic which swept through Britain in the early 1970s the case of Mr Robert Keenan has an important place. On the night of 5 November 1972 Mr Keenan was walking home after a few drinks in Handsworth, Birmingham when he was stopped by three youths and asked for a cigarette. While his attention was diverted he was knocked down and dragged to a piece of waste ground. There he was robbed and badly beaten. One of his attackers apparently hit him with a brick while the others kicked him as he lay on the ground. As a consequence of this assault it was feared that Mr Keenan might suffer permanent physical and mental damage. More than five months after the attack he was still receiving hospital treatment and quite unable to resume his job as a building worker. The three youths involved eventually admitted their guilt and were given long sentences. The ringleader, who was 16 years old, was ordered to be detained for 20 years. His two 15-year-old friends were each sentenced to 10 years.[1] These harsh and exemplary sentences, like those passed on the Great Train Robbers in 1964, were justified mainly in terms of their general deterrent effect. That is, other potential muggers and train robbers would be deterred, or so it was argued, from committing similar crimes for fear of receiving equally harsh treatment.

One of the main purposes of the penal system, then, is seen to be deterrence. In theory, as in the cases just cited, the tougher the punishment the greater the deterrence. This is a view shared by many judges and the press and probably by most members of the public too. The difficulty is that not only is such a claim hard to verify, but also what evidence there is tends to suggest that potential offenders are more likely to be deterred by fear of being caught than by fear of the punishment they might receive, however great. The harsh sentences handed out for the mugging of Mr Robert

Keenan are a case in point. A survey carried out by two Home Office research workers based on six large urban police areas came to the conclusion that these sentences had hardly any impact on the overall level of recorded muggings. What it did find, however, was a close correlation in some areas between a decline in muggings and the introduction of positive police measures, such as more special patrols. In other words, where the fear of detection increased so the level of muggings fell.[2]

To be sure, the overall evidence about deterrence is far from complete and it is difficult to believe that it does not have at least a modest part to play in one context or another. However, the easy assurance with which it is called upon to justify sometimes severe exemplary sentences is surely open to serious doubts. Equally questionable is the idea of reform or, in the language of the 1960s, rehabilitation. What this suggests is that offenders somehow become 'better people' as a result of their experiences in the penal system, whether it is time spent on probation or a spell in prison or Borstal. They have time to reflect or be 'treated', the upshot of which is a determination to keep the social contract, to 'live by the rules'. For the progressive wing of the penal lobby this reforming process has long been seen as the primary purpose of the penal system. Unfortunately there is not much evidence to suggest that many offenders are, in fact, reformed in this way. Why offenders do eventually decide to 'go straight' is difficult to ascertain, but it probably has more to do with wider social factors, say the chance of a good job or settling down to start a family, than to their experience within the penal system. Of course, it is arguable that individual offenders are deterred by their experience of prison, and resolve never to go back there. But this, as Jeremy Bentham reminds us, is not reform: 'If the delinquent, after he has been punished, is only deterred by fear from the repetition of his offence, he is not reformed. Reformation implies a change of character and moral dispositions.'[3]

Lack of confidence in the penal system as a means of securing general deterrence or reform has taken the penal lobby back to basics. Increasingly the penal system is seen by the lobby to be about punishment. This changing emphasis, once perceived, will be supported by the public which has consistently taken the main purpose of the penal system to be about punishment, even when the reform or rehabilitative ideal was at its height in the late 1950s and 1960s. The fact that this ideal was shared, in part anyway, by both the major parliamentary parties gave the politics of penal reform during that period the appearance of being more of a tension between Parliament and people than an ideological struggle between Labour and Conservatives. This parliamentary consensus, the wish to treat penal policy in a non-partisan way, proved highly durable, as we shall see, and in some quarters even survived the law-and-order debate of the 1970s and the transition from rehabilitation to punishment.

The public's continuing support for a penal system which is more about punishment than rehabilitation may not mean that all attempts to make the system less harsh will be scoffed at, dismissed by a punishment-crazed public. For instance, the evidence of a recent opinion poll showed that while a majority of the public wanted to continue with tougher penalties for violent crimes, there was a wide measure of support for more use to be made of non-custodial measures for other types of crime normally punishable by imprisonment, say burglary.[4] Some commentators see this tendency towards 'bifurcation' as the future direction of penal policy, though they are not all convinced that this will amount to a more liberal regime, particularly for those left on the inside. They could all too easily come to be seen as the 'bottom of the barrel', prisoners on whom any sort of indignity might be heaped, including drug-induced behavioural changes.

To talk about the purposes of the penal system in terms of reform or punishment is ultimately to engage in the language of moral philosophy. Such language has its place, indeed it is through these or allied concepts such as retribution or deterrence that most people traditionally come to understand and justify the penal system. However, such language tells us very little about the specific shape of any given penal system, or why and how it changes; about why, say, some punishments popular in the eighteenth century are no longer in use, or vice versa. To achieve this sort of understanding requires a more obviously material and historical approach. Take, for example, the modern prison, which in its present form is less than 200 years old.

During the eighteenth century exceptional measures were taken to deal with the struggle between cottagers and gentry over customary rights. One of these measures, the Black Act, made the already draconian criminal law tougher still by greatly increasing the number of capital offences. This met with opposition. Juries refused to convict people whom they thought might be hanged for relatively minor offences. Judges also shied away from passing the death sentence and many offenders were sentenced to transportation instead. General dissatisfaction with the criminal law and the penal code grew and there were demonstrations, even riots, at public hangings and whippings. The ending of transportation and the creation of the 'urban masses' as a consequence of industrialisation made the situation even more volatile. It was the pressure of these events that helped to make imprisonment a regular and widely used punishment, and the modern prison as we understand it came into being. Punishment was no longer meted out before an audience, as a public demonstration of social and political authority, but in secret, behind closed doors. The prison rather than the public gallows or the pillory became the new symbol of social control.

This historical perspective is important to any proper understanding of the penal system for at least two reasons. In the first place, and with particular reference to our enterprise, it clearly demonstrates that to talk about the penal system since 1945 is to consider a very short moment indeed. The forces that have been crucial in shaping the present system lie much further back in time. Second, history reminds us that change is not only possible but likely, so there is no reason to believe that prisons, or Borstals for that matter, just because we have become used to them will go on for ever: alternative forms of punishment are possible. It is important, though, not to see all change as progress. This is a blindness which afflicts all social engineers, penal reformers no less than others. Take, for example, the suggestion by two American criminologists that we might soon be in a position to implant telemetric devices into an offender's body so that his location and emotional state can be centrally monitored. The idea behind this frightening suggestion is presumably that it would allow potentially 'dangerous' offenders to serve their time more usefully, and safely, in the community at less cost to the taxpayer. But could such an alternative to prison reasonably be described as progress? The question has to be asked, even when the alternatives on offer are far less obviously alarming, as we shall see in Part Three.

If our understanding of the penal system is enlarged by history, so it can also benefit from recent sociological perspectives on deviancy which have helped to stand traditional criminology on its head. Instead of concentrating on the law-breaker and searching for correctional techniques, sociologists have shifted their attention to the law-making process itself. This has raised some central, if obvious, questions, such as why are some actions in society which are clearly injurious to large numbers of people not subject to the criminal law and penal sanction while others are? And who decides? Who makes the criminal law and decides the penal code? Not all groups in society have the same power in this respect, any more than there is universal agreement about what actions should or should not be criminalised. Suspicions about this power differential and what it might mean are reinforced by the knowledge that it is mainly the poor and the underprivileged who are subject to the harsh end of the penal system, who now inhabit our chronically overcrowded and sometimes brutal prisons. All these concerns obviously try to locate the penal system in a wider network of social and power relations, an approach which only connects indirectly, if at all, with the language of moral philosophy.

These sociological perspectives on deviancy had some impact in the 1970s with the creation of pressure groups like Radical Alternatives to Prison (RAP) and the prisoners' union, PROP. However, what is surprising is just how little impact they had on the policies and attitudes of the Labour Party, which continued to see penal policy as somehow being 'above politics'. Indeed, between 1974 and 1979 the Conservative Party in opposition was roundly condemned for making law and order into a 'political issue', and the Labour Government sought to demonstrate that it could be just as tough on criminals as the Tories, an approach which both perplexed and distressed some of the Labour Party's rank and file. These various tensions both within and between the parties have not been resolved by any means, and with the Conservative Government again putting law and order high on the political agenda it is important to understand why the one-time parliamentary consensus on penal policy eventually came under attack.

REFERENCES

1. S. HALL *et al.*, *Policing the Crisis* (Macmillan: London, 1978) Ch. 4.
2. *New Society*, 2 Jan. 1975.
3. J. BENTHAM, *Collected Works* (Bowring: Edinburgh, 1843) p. 404.
4. *The Observer*, 2 March 1982.

Part one
THE CONTEXT

Chapter one

REFORM 1945–1959

Makers of penal policy were optimistic in the 1930s. The daily average prison population of England and Wales was proportionately one of the lowest prison populations in the world, and the success of the Borstal system in turning young offenders away from crime was singled out for particular praise. In this mood of optimism the Conservative Government introduced the Criminal Justice Bill in 1938. It was widely welcomed as a major and progressive piece of penal legislation but as it happened, this Bill never reached the statute book. The Second World War intervened, and when it was reintroduced as a Labour Government Bill in 1947 the climate of opinion was far less optimistic. The reason for this change is easily explained. Between 1939 and 1945 the number of indictable offences, and of persons convicted of them, increased by 50 per cent. This placed a heavy burden on the penal system, especially the prison service. By 1945 the daily average prison population had reached nearly 15,000, a huge increase over the immediate prewar figure of between 10,000 and 11,000. Nor was the worst yet over. The rate of recorded crime continued to rise after the war, albeit unevenly, until 1951 and the prison population peaked at just over 25,000 in 1952, which at that time was the highest figure for the present century.

In these circumstances the Criminal Justice Bill 1947 not surprisingly turned out to be tougher than its prewar counterpart. For example, although the Labour Bill retained the clause to abolish corporal punishment as a sentence of the court, it was felt necessary, as a *quid pro quo* to those like Lord Chief Justice Goddard who felt that this was no time to be 'going soft', to introduce detention centres where young offenders were to be given a 'short, sharp shock'. These centres were to be purely punitive and Labour's Home Secretary firmly resisted the idea that they should develop anything other than a brisk, military-style regime. The normal period of detention was to be three months. Perhaps because of financial stringency not many of these centres were actually opened in the first half of the 1950s, but their essentially negative regime soon became known.

Labour's Bill can be seen as still tougher in other respects. For example, whereas the original 1938 Bill had placed a complete ban on imprisoning young offenders under 16 the revised Bill lowered this to 15 for higher courts. Further, the maximum period of preventive detention was raised from 10 to 14 years, a very substantial increase. It is important to stress, however, that although these changes, if taken together with certain other provisions in the 1947 Bill, do genuinely reflect a 'get tough' attitude, the main rationale of penal policy was to a large extent unshaken by the public anxiety which surrounded a rising crime rate. That is, in the immediate postwar period the Home Office and Prison Commission still believed – as did important pressure groups like the Howard League – that those who had transgressed the law could be reformed and, in particular, that there were available or devisable institutional regimes which could, to quote the Prison Rules (1949–56), train prisoners to 'live a good and useful life on discharge'.

Consider, for example, what the 1947 Bill provided for in respect of Borstal. As mentioned earlier, the Borstal system won particular praise between the wars when under the guidance of Sir Alexander Paterson it achieved good results. This success owed something, it was argued, to the very real effort that had been made to provide a range of different Borstal institutions to suit the varying needs and abilities of young offenders. Above all, the real strength of the system was seen to be its emphasis on character training, the belief that the regime must be based on 'progressive trust demanding increasing personal decision, responsibility and self-control'.[1] The framework for achieving this was to be the house system and a day built around hard physical work, vocational training, education and a strong moral atmosphere. What the 1947 Bill provided for was the extension of this positive and apparently reforming experience to more young offenders. Eligibility for Borstal training had been restricted previously to those who had already formed 'criminal habits'. Now it was to be available to any young offender whom the courts felt might benefit from the experience.

A further illustration of the commitment to the potential of reform can be seen in the Bill's provision for persistent adult offenders. Two sentences were involved, corrective training, which was new, and preventive detention. What is important here is that although different regimes were devised, in theory at least, for these separate categories of persistent offender, both were geared to the potential of reform. Even the 'incorrigible' preventive detainee was expected to respond to his positive training, though it might take many years, and the rate of progress vary from prisoner to prisoner.

In addition to this confidence in reform the Labour Government also took the view that the rising crime rate was a temporary phenomenon. During and immediately after the war, family life had been disrupted and the bonds of traditional social discipline loosened. Once things 'settled down', when the troops returned home and normal family life was resumed, discipline would be restored. This was an assessment shared by many Conservatives too. A second and related point was the belief that shortages had helped to push up the crime rate. Labour hoped that once these shortages had been eliminated, when the black market and the 'spivs' who operated it became redundant, then the plague of widespread 'fiddling' would come to an end. Also, of course, although Labour did not exactly equate crime with poverty, many took the not unreasonable view that at least some of the poor were driven into crime by economic neessity, from the pressure of 'making ends meet'. The Welfare State which Labour was building, the centrepiece of its postwar political achievement, was going to get rid of this pressure. In a society where all had sufficient the need to resort to crime must surely be lessened. For all these reasons then, although Labour's Criminal Justice Bill 1947 was indeed tough, it was by no means desperate.

CAPITAL PUNISHMENT

For the many thousands who were to be processed through the penal system in the 1950s the provisions of the Criminal Justice Bill 1947 outlined above were to have very real and often harsh consequences. Yet the main provisions of the Bill received only modest press coverage. What gripped the public imagination instead was the attempt to write into the Bill a clause to abolish capital punishment. The struggle to abolish capital punishment before the war had rested largely with the National Council for the Abolition of the Death Penalty under the guidance of Roy Calvert. Although some progress had been made in educating influential opinion Parliament still had many doubts, and it therefore came as no great surprise to find that the Criminal Justice Bill 1938 contained no commitment to abolition. Perhaps more surprising was that Labour's postwar Bill took the same line. After all, the Labour Party had passed an abolitionist motion at its 1934 conference, and it was well known that there were many abolitionists in the 1945 parliamentary Party. Why Labour soft-pedalled on this issue may be explained, in part at least, by the attitude of Home Secretary Chuter Ede. Although at one time in favour of abolition, Ede was by 1947 firmly against it, having been influenced in this direction by senior Home Office civil servants, particularly Sir Frank Newsam. In short, there was a departmental view against abolition and Ede had been persuaded to accept it. It was in an attempt to get round this opposition that the Howard League helped to organise a petition to the Home Secretary which was signed by nearly 200 MPs. This had no discernible impact on Chuter Ede and a deputation from the National Council for the Abolition of the Death Penalty was equally unsuccessful. There were, however, limits to the Home Secretary's authority, and it later became clear that the Government would face a sizeable backbench revolt over the issue. Chuter Ede was therefore forced to agree to Sidney Silverman's motion – to suspend the death penalty for five years – being debated on a free vote when the Bill eventually came back to the floor of the House on report. This was the signal for a large-scale lobby. Sensing that victory might be near, the National Council was particularly active, supplying MPs from all sides with statistics and argument. No MP was ignored in the struggle over Silverman's abolition clause which was finally debated on 15th April 1948. The floor of the House was packed, the public and press galleries overflowing.

Silverman spoke first and, with Christopher Hollis, the Conservative MP chosen to second the abolition clause, and contributions from many other supporters in the House, the arguments against capital punishment were duly covered. Was the death penalty really a deterrent to murder? Was it not possible to make an error, were not innocent men hanged? Was the judicial right to take life morally justified? There were a number of speeches against the clause. Quintin Hogg (later Lord Chancellor) used the somewhat eccentric argument that as we had agreed to the death penalty at the Nuremberg trials, to disown it now would dishonour the House. Chuter Ede, the final speaker against the clause, argued that it would be foolish to change the law at a time when crimes of violence were on the increase. Further, and clearly an argument directed at his own Party, he claimed that many working-class people were set against abolition and that it would be wrong on an issue of this kind to ignore such strong sentiments. The final minutes of the debate were dramatic. Retentionists had frequently used Sir Alexander Paterson's much respected opinion that long-term imprisonment was so inhumane that capital punishment was to be preferred. Speaking last, Reginald Paget, a member of the Howard League, claimed that while this may have been Paterson's view in 1930, improvements in the prison regime had led him to re-consider his decision and shortly before his death in 1947 he had joined the abolitionists. As it turned out, this was a mistake, and Paget was roundly condemned by the retentionists who argued that his intervention had been decisive. This seems unlikely, though it may have had some small effect in securing what was, by any stan-dards, a dramatic victory for the abolitionists by 247 votes to 224. Not surprisingly, whereas the Labour Party came out strongly in favour of abolition with 215 votes, the number of Conservative Party abolitionists only amounted to 14. On the opposite side, the Conservative Party voted 134 for retention to the Labour Party's 74.

Of course, the issue was far from settled. The clause had yet to be considered by the Lords, who were known to be hostile. Although not wishing to be seen as in any way acting unfairly against a Labour Government which had received such a decisive majority in 1945, the Lords felt that they had public opinion on their side. The available evidence supported that view: a Gallup Poll taken shortly after the Commons vote showed that the public were decisively against abolition and that this was an opinion shared by people of all age groups and socio-economic classes. Fortified by evidence like this the Lords hurled themselves against the clause. Much was made of the fact that the Law Lords opposed it, and Lord Chief Justice Goddard made what can best be described as one of the most grisly speeches ever to have been made in the Lords during its very long history. The Bishop of Truro was hardly less temperate by suggesting that the death penalty should actually be extended to cover cases of *attempted* murder. In the face of such fierce and at times hysterical opposition the abolitionists were never likely to win, and although Lord Templewood put up a reasoned defence of the clause the vote was a foregone conclusion. Silver-man's measure was thrown out by a huge majority, 181 votes to 28. Only one bishop voted in favour of abolition. For the Lords this was a fairly large turnout; the backwoodsmen had made their mark.

The Lords' decision fairly obviously placed the Labour Govern-ment in an embarrassing position. Although not in favour of the abolition clause as a government, it was obliged to pursue the 'expressed wishes of the House'. Thus it was in a far from enthusiastic mood that it brought forward a compromise clause which it hoped both Houses would agree to pass. What the new proposal did in very simple terms was to draw a distinction between types of murder – for some murders the death penalty would be available, for others not. This proposal ran into serious difficulties. In the first place, it was not at all the complete ban that Silverman with his supporters had won just a few weeks before. They were forced to accept it, but they remained unenthusiastic. Second, the distinctions it tried to draw would inevitably give rise to curious anomalies, and Churchill ridiculed the proposal when it came before the Commons, thus helping to turn it into a Party issue. It did pass, though, under the discipline of the Whips, but only to be thrown out again by the Lords where even Lord Templewood announced his intention to vote against it.

The Labour Government was now in a very tight corner. Because the clause in dispute was not part of the original Bill, and because of a shortage of time, the Government could not out-flank the Lords by invoking the Parliament Act. This left the possibility of carrying on the fight into the next session. The Government was reluctant – the planned schedule was already heavy and the Criminal Justice Bill might get squeezed out altogether. Given the important changes that the Bill proposed for the penal system as a whole, this was a possibility that the Government felt unable to accept. The abolition clause was therefore dropped from the Bill. The retentionists had won an important victory.

After the defeat of its compromise clause in 1948 the Labour Government set up a Royal Commission to 'consider and report whether liability under the criminal law in Great Britain to suffer capital punishment for murder should be limited or modified . . .'. Abolition was thus specifically ruled out, and this probably reflected the Labour Government's belief that whereas the struggle over the Silverman clause had shown that there was no parliamentary majority for abolition, there was nonetheless pressure for some change. The Royal Commission Report of 1953 contained several interesting recommendations, not least the suggestion that juries should be empowered in each case to decide whether life imprisonment could properly be substituted for the death penalty. This recommendation plus others, like those which touched on the thorny question of how to assess the murderer's 'state of mind' at the time, and how this might reasonably be taken into account when assessing his degree of 'responsibility', were widely debated in the press and helped to keep the question of capital punishment before the public. However, what really concentrated the public mind was a succession of murder trials involving Bentley and Craig, Evans and Christie, and Ruth Ellis. No one who lived through the 1950s is ever likely to forget these names.

In 1952 Derek Bentley, aged 19, and Christopher Craig, aged 16, were discovered while committing robbery. In the course of their arrest a policeman was killed. Craig fired the shot at a time when Bentley had already been caught and was in police custody. As he was under the legal age for hanging (18), Craig was sentenced to life imprisonment but Bentley, in spite of public protests and considerable effort by leading political figures such as Aneurin Bevan, was hanged. These bald facts were hedged around by certain complications, but not enough to alter the public feeling that Bentley had been harshly treated by being judged according to the doctrine of constructive malice which made him, in the eyes of the law, as guilty as Craig of the unfortunate policeman's death. (The Royal Commission called for the abolition of the doctrine of constructive malice which meant, in effect, that a person involved in a common purpose with others must assume common responsibility for anything that happens in pursuit of that purpose.) The case of Evans and Christie was more complicated and more horrific. Briefly, Evans confessed to the police that he had killed his wife. Police searched his family home and discovered not only the body of his wife but the body of his murdered daughter also. Evans later denied murdering his wife, claiming that the murderer was in fact John Christie, an ex-policeman who also lived in the same house. In the event, Evans was charged with his daughter's murder, found guilty – with Christie acting as a witness for the prosecution – and hanged in 1950. Three years later the popular dailies erupted with the news that the bodies of six woman had been found in John Christie's flat. Under investigation Christie admitted killing Mrs Evans but not her daughter. Public pressure forced the Home Secretary to appoint a one-man inquiry into the case. The main question troubling the public conscience was, had Evans been wrongly convicted of his daughter's murder? The inquiry, conducted with great speed, reached the conclusion that not only had Evans been justly hanged for that murder, but that he had also murdered his wife in spite of Christie's confession. This conclusion was never fully accepted by the public, and the anxiety that Evans might have been unjustly hanged lingered on. A great injustice, too, was thought to have been done to Ruth Ellis, though for different reasons. No one doubted that Ellis had shot her lover, but it seems certain that she was in a far from balanced state of mind when the offence was committed. The mother of two children, badly treated by her lovers, Ruth Ellis attracted much public sympathy, and when she was found guilty a petition for her reprieve was sent to the Home Secretary. It was ignored, however, and large crowds gathered outside Holloway prison on the morning of her execution in 1955.

Cases like these began to force the pace for abolition and in 1955 Victor Gollancz, Arthur Koestler and Canon John Collins founded the National Campaign for the Abolition of the Death Penalty. The case for such a widely based strategy rested mainly on the abolitionists' belief that unless outside pressure was brought to bear, Parliament would not vote to change the *status quo*. For example, the debate on the Royal Commission had been purposely delayed by the Conservative Government under Churchill for over a year and Silverman's abolition amendment linked to that debate had been defeated without difficulty. Further, as if to confirm the National Council's strategy, the newly-elected Conservative Government (1955) also turned out to be lukewarm about the Royal Commission's proposals and just as far from abolition as its predecessor. It was against this impasse that the nation-wide activities of the Council were directed. There were soon branches in Scotland, Sheffield, Birmingham and Leeds, and books like Arthur Koestler's *Reflections on Hanging* (1956) were published at an accessible price by Gollancz and widely read. It was, partly, the success of this campaign that helped to persuade the Conservative Government that the issue had to be raised yet again, and in 1956 it brought forward a motion which, while against abolition, advocated change in the law relating to murder. The Government hoped that this tactic would out-flank the abolitionists. Realising exactly what the Government was up to, the abolitionists tacked on their own amendment, and it was carried with the help of 48 Conservative votes.

The Government's response to this embarrassing defeat was to agree to allow time for a Private Member's Bill to come before the House in favour of abolition, and for it to be decided upon by a free vote. Silverman duly obliged and, accompanied by much extra-parliamentary support orchestrated by the National Council, the Bill was eventually passed by the Commons in July 1956. But what of the Lords, how would they react? They were in no doubt, throwing the Bill out by 238 votes to 85. This again was a huge turnout, even higher than in 1948. People genuinely wondered who these people were and where they had come from. The anger which underpinned this sense of wonder helped to convince the Conservative Government that, although not itself in favour of abolition, some compromise had to be found. The Lords could not go on rejecting Bills on this subject, especially as there was some suggestion that public opinion was on the turn, and to be forced into sidestepping the Lords' delaying powers was not a move any Conservative Government would relish. What the Conservative Cabinet came up with – and it was a compromise which suited most of the members well enough – was a Bill in two parts. The first part amended the existing law on murder, abolishing, for example, the doctrine of constructive malice which had helped to seal Derek Bentley's fate. The second part divided murders into capital and non-capital murders, the former to carry the death penalty while the latter would not. This distinction, as Churchill had pointed out in 1948, would give rise to all sorts of inconsistencies. This clearly worried retentionists and abolitionists alike but the Government refused to be moved by these anxieties. The abolitionists were particularly bitter. The Bill was far from what they had worked for. However, their parliamentary manoeuvrings came to nothing and the Bill passed both Houses unamended to become the Homicide Act in March 1957.

The struggle to abolish the death penalty dominated penal reform in the ten years or so after the war. True, other issues like corporal punishment occasionally captured the headlines, but no other issue aroused the same intense emotions as the death penalty. Clearly, very ordinary people felt quite rightly that their moral perspective was as valid as anyone else's, and in this they were sustained by the popular press which continually came back to the central arguments. For MPs, too, it was a matter of high principle, and one Labour member insisted on being carried through the abolitionist lobby on a stretcher. If abolitionists like Silverman and his supporters outside Parliament in the National Campaign were disappointed with the Homicide Act 1957, their criticisms of it were to prove right and the struggle for total abolition was soon to resume. The fight was far from over.

THE SYSTEM UNDER STRAIN

Implementing the provisions of the Criminal Justice Act 1948 was no easy task. The overcrowding which took place during and after the war threw the prison system out of balance. Towards the end of the war the number of young people sentenced to Borstal training began to grow rapidly, and the only way the Prison Commission could cope with this expansion was by overcrowding local prisons. At one stage this meant placing 6,000 prisoners three to a cell, and this number only dropped gradually to 3,000 by 1955. This difficult situation was aggravated initially by staff shortages. For prison officers newly recruited to the service this meant a reduced period of basic training, while for some prisoners the working week had to be reduced to twenty-five hours.

Conditions continued to be difficult for the Borstal system too, though this can by no means be blamed entirely on the 1948 Act's provision to widen the Borstal constituency. The problem has its roots further back. At the start of the war in 1939 all senior Borstal detainees were released overnight, and most of the staff soon disappeared. Thus, when Borstal receptions began to increase towards the end of the war there was a shortage, not only of accommodation but also of experienced staff to maintain the traditions which had been established during the 1930s. The pressure continued after the war, and in 1952 the Borstal population was approaching 4,000. Given these difficulties it is not surprising that the success rate of Borstal, measured in terms of reconviction rates, was well down, though the Prison Commission continued to have faith in Borstal training and by the mid-1950s was claiming that the system was just about back to its prewar best. This was not a view that was shared by everyone, by any means.

Detention centres had no tradition to build on, but they soon satisfied the Prison Commission by developing a regime of 'strict discipline and high tempo' which, in spite of the *Daily Herald's* campaign to discredit it, was very popular with magistrates who only wished for something even tougher. They thought their hopes were about to be fulfilled early in 1953 when a Conservative backbencher tabled a Private Member's Bill to reintroduce corporal punishment. Pressure for this had been building up for some months: a Gallup Poll in November 1952 had shown that 31 per cent of the people interviewed thought that corporal punishment with short terms of imprisonment was the best way of dealing with offenders who committed crimes of violence. This was an opinion publicly endorsed yet again by Lord Chief Justice Goddard at about the same time. The Howard League for Penal Reform campaigned against the Bill, largely to counter the Magistrates Association which published the results of a referendum among its own members. The magistrates' vote in favour of corporal punishment, as the Howard League dryly observed at the time, might just have been influenced by a leaflet accompanying the ballot forms which proclaimed that 'Children of an atomic age require robust treatment'! On the Government side, the parliamentary argument was conducted in an altogether fairer and more dispassionate way and the then Conservative Home Secretary had no trouble in persuading the House to reject the Bill; though not before the Bill's sponsor had the chance to read from one of his supporters' letters which expressed the hope that the Home Secretary and members of the Howard League might get coshed before the Bill was presented! Again, it is important to balance this somewhat ferocious attitude with more constructive approaches, such as that of the Maxwell Committee on aftercare which reported in the same year, 1953. This recommended that since material benefits were now available to discharged prisoners through the newly created Welfare State, voluntary aid societies should reduce their activity in this area and try to find other ways, on a casework basis, of trying to help individual prisoners adjust to freedom.

On the question of welfare, the Prison Officers Association (POA) also claimed an interest. There was, for example, the Norwich experiment which in the mid-1950s was much praised by the Howard League. This involved certain changes in the established prison routine such as removing the officers' raised surveillance platforms from prison workshops, greater association for prisoners at mealtimes and, in particular, prison officers were encouraged to write short reports on those prisoners in their charge to assist local aid societies. This reflected the prison officer's belief that he was more than just a turnkey. And it must be said, in the period 1945– 59 such a belief was not unreasonable. The idea of reform, and of the reforming process, was not widely thought of as belonging to the complicated mysteries of the social sciences. On the contrary, it was to be achieved through an old-fashioned mixture of firm discipline, hard work and learning by example. The prison officer's role in this process was, as the Prison Commission itself was so fond of arguing, crucial:

the chief hope of importing a new direction and purpose to the lives of . . . prisoners lies in the bearing and example of all members of the prison staff and their personal influence on individual prisoners. It is the business of the staff to know and understand the men under their charge as individual human beings, to discover what is good for them and to develop the good to beat the bad . . .[2]

The POA maintained that it was this vital and positive role, among other things, which entitled them to higher status and better pay. The Prison Commission did not agree, and annual pay negotiations went to arbitration no less than six times during the 1950s.

Needless to say, it was not all welfare and reform and there were occasional allegations concerning the ill-treatment of prisoners by warders. One incident raised in the Commons by Labour MP Bessie Braddock during the mid-1950s is of particular interest for at least two reasons. First, the subsequent inquiry was carried out by an independent person, not the sort of procedure adopted in recent years where the Home Office prefers to send in its own man. Second, the inquiry found allegations against two prison officers proved, and the Prison Commission recommended that they should be dismissed from the service. However, after personal hearings both were reinstated. How far, it was asked, might the Home Office be pushed by the POA if the going really got tough?

Of the ill-treatment that was meted out in the 1950s not too much was directed at IRA prisoners. That at least was Sean Macstiofain's experience: born in England, Macstiofain eventually became the IRA's Chief of Staff. He was arrested in 1953 with three other Republicans and spent all of his sentence in Wormwood Scrubs, which at that time also contained a number of Greek Cypriots who had been imprisoned by the British for offences committed in Cyprus during the Emergency. Although not subjected to any severe physical abuse, it seems that Republican prisoners suffered the usual prison frustrations – delayed mail, censorship – more than most. Their situation was somewhat improved, suggests Macstiofain, by the arrival of a new governor who was sympathetic to their claim to be political prisoners and who subsequently put them in cells next to each other. (For another view, see Brendan Behan's *Borstal Boy*.)

The number of people found guilty of indictable offences began to rise from 1956 onwards. As a consequence the pressure on the prison system, which had eased a little after 1952, began to intensify. The population of prisons and Borstals at the start of 1956 was 21,000; by the beginning of 1959 it was running at over 26,000. The Approved School system was also under pressure; a population of 6,800 in January 1956 had turned into 7,800 three years later. It was with these figures very much in mind that the Government was pleased to welcome the First Offenders Bill 1958 when it was introduced into the Commons by George Benson, backbencher and chairman of the Howard League. The Criminal Justice Act 1948 had stipulated that before an adolescent could be sentenced to imprisonment the court must first consider alternative types of sentence. Prison was not ruled out, but reasons had to be given why alternative sentences were not thought suitable. Initially this provision had some success in diverting adolescents from prison and Benson's Bill was designed to extend the provision to adult first offenders.

The sort of situation which was made worse by the growing pressure of numbers occurred at Carlton House in 1959. Carlton House was a senior boys Approved School with a regime thought suitable for the more 'robust and vigorous' type of boy. During two days in August there were 'serious disturbances' at the school. The boys refused to work, some absconded, windows were broken and debris strewn around. The staff lost control altogether and when appeals for order from the managers were slow to take effect, the police moved in to take control. The disturbances were reported in the national press and the whole affair became something of a *cause célèbre*.

A number of boys were duly punished for their actions, but the real blame for the disturbances was eventually placed where it properly belonged, on the shoulders of the headmaster and the school managers who had ignored important recommendations from the Home Office Inspectorate about how the organisation of the school could be improved. However, much was made during the inquiry of the recent difficulties faced by Carlton House. It was pointed out that because of the increased numbers of boys being sent to senior Approved Schools, Carlton House had been forced to increase its intake by over 10 per cent in July 1958, even though there were real doubts as to whether the school could cope with such an increase. Anxieties were also expressed about the type of boy being sent to Carlton House. Instead of being willing and compliant the typical boy was now agressive and unwilling to accept the level of discipline which the masters demanded. Their anxieties – and they were expressed by those who ran the Borstal system too – were common in the second half of the 1950s. They reflect the moral panic which greeted the rise of a postwar generation identified with Elvis Presley and Gene Vincent, the so-called delinquent generation symbolised by the Teddy boy in his drainpipe trousers and drape jacket. The disciplinary society seemed unable to cope. Institutions of social control which had succeeded in the past now seemed open to question and the response of the Carlton House inquiry with its proposals for a secure Approved School and the provision of 'strong rooms' for containing difficult boys was a fairly typical – if *ad hoc* – response to a situation which many people felt was getting 'out of hand', and which had been deteriorating since the mid-1950s.

That the public should have reacted to the growth in crime during the second half of the 1950s with such a sense of bewilderment, even panic, is hardly surprising. After all, society seemed less divided than in the past, the Welfare State was firmly established, the consumer boom in full swing and few doubted Harold Macmillan's 1959 election-winning slogan that 'You've never had it so good'. In such a buoyant, stable and affluent society why was it that more and more people, particularly young people, were breaking the law? Labour politicians found this question particularly difficult to answer. In the main, they came to rely on Tawney's idea of the acquisitive society. This, it was argued, produced a 'get-rich-quick' mentality which encouraged people to pursue 'success' at any cost and by any route. Conservatives on the other hand put more stress on the family. Too many mothers were now going out to work, society had produced a generation of under-disciplined 'latchkey' children. To be sure, this was only one (as we shall see in Part Two) of the many explanations put forward by the Conservatives as they, like Labour, struggled to understand this complex social 'mystery'.

PENAL PRACTICE IN A CHANGING SOCIETY

In this atmosphere of increasing concern the public began to demand to know what action the Home Secretary was going to take. The answer was spelt out in a government White Paper, *Penal Practice in a Changing Society* (Cmnd 645) which was published in 1959. The White Paper began by accepting that the rising crime rate, particularly among the young, was a proper matter for public concern, and it then went on to outline a threefold strategy to deal with it. First, there were the police. Their role in preventing crime was seen as crucial, and the White Paper made it clear that the Government expected the police to tighten up their operations. What the Government had in mind was better communication between neighbouring forces and greater use of cars, motor-cycles and communication systems, all designed to keep track of an increasingly mobile criminal fraternity. The Panda car and two-way radios were on their way.

The second aspect of the Government's strategy concerned the criminal law. The view that only tough sentences would deter serious crime was accepted. However, it was pointed out that existing penalties – in spite of what the public believed – were already tough. Capital punishment still existed; life imprisonment was available for manslaughter, rape and robbery with violence; and many forms of larceny could be punishable by up to fourteen years imprisonment. On this score at least, the criminal law was adequate. Not so satisfactory, though, was the ability of some criminals to escape just punishment through defects in the law. To remedy this a Standing Committee on Criminal Law Revision was to be appointed to close some of the loopholes. Prompt action was also needed to improve the efficiency of the courts. Particular anxiety was felt over the time taken to bring people to trial, and whether or not magistrates and judges really knew enough about offenders who came before them to select the most appropriate sentences. It was all a matter of timing, and the White Paper referred to a committee under Mr Justice Streatfeild which had been appointed to look into this very question, with the promise that its recommendations would receive immediate consideration.

Finally, the main thrust of the White Paper was directed at the penal system itself, and how it might contribute to the struggle against crime. The argument developed in the White Paper needs close attention since it was apparently contradictory. To start with, and hardly surprisingly, much was made of overcrowding. It was pointed out that detention centres were so full that magistrates had been prevented from using them as alternatives to short-term imprisonment. Borstal overcrowding had meant young offenders sometimes had to wait up to twelve months before a suitable vacancy could be found. The situation was so bad that during the course of the previous year four prisons had been turned into Borstals and two more Borstals had been fashioned out of redundant service camps. Local prisons too, were suffering, with cell-sharing again on the increase.

These very practical constraints led to the obvious question: could the prison system, faced with such overcrowding, reasonably be expected to reform the criminal, to persuade him on discharge to 'lead a good and useful life'? The answer was, no. The prison system had its successes, of course, but too many prisoners were reconvicted again and again, and in this sense the penal system was not playing its full part in the struggle against crime. At an obvious level this could be put right by providing more prison facilities to reduce overcrowding. The White Paper stated the case for this and spelt out the details of its current building programme. Six more detention centres were to be available. These centres were regarded as a great success. The White Paper pointed out that their purely 'negative' approach had been modified. The 'short, sharp shock' was being combined with more positive training and these centres now had 'a legitimate place in a variegated system of treatment for young offenders'. The Borstal system was to be expanded too. There were to be several new secure Borstals for boys, one for girls, and another Borstal reception centre where trainees would go for observation and classification. A plan to rebuild local prisons to a more acceptable standard was also mentioned, while untried prisoners, and those who had been tried but were awaiting classification, would be housed away from local prisons – so reducing their population – in purpose-built observation and classifying centres. In the long term there were plans to rebuild both Dartmoor and Holloway.

The confidence with which the White Paper announced this commitment to more and more institutional training is surely questionable. Were existing methods of training, even if carried on in less crowded conditions, so successful as to justify this expansion? There was certainly room for doubt. For example, the detention centre regime continued to be attacked. The White Paper might claim that research showed them a success, that their regime was now less punitive, but the research was far from conclusive, and many informed sources considered that they were still run on lines which contradicted the very principles of training for reform. Clearly, the 'success' of the detention experiment has to be explained in other ways, and Hilary Land is surely right when she observes[3]:

The development of detention centres depended little on whether they were judged to be a 'success' or 'failure'. The evaluation of their effect on young offenders was interpreted in the most optimistic light by the Prison Commissioners because, at the end of the fifties, they needed a relatively cheap and quick method of expanding custodial training to meet the increasing demands that the rising crime rate was making on their penal institutions; magistrates were determined to use them whatever the research findings said and ten weeks in a detention centre was considered preferable to corporal punishment or a short spell in prison. In this sense detention centres were an experiment which could not be allowed to fail.

To an extent, the same sort of justification was also applied to Borstal. The results of Borstal training since the war had been far from encouraging. By the late 1950s many young offenders found its paternalistic and sometimes harsh regime difficult to stomach, and although the Prison Commission continued to publicise its alleged virtues, Alan Sillitoe's *The Loneliness of the Long-distance Runner* (1959) is a more accurate picture of what was really happening inside Borstals at this time than a whole truckload of Commission pamphlets. But, so the argument went, a spell in Borstal was at least better than a prison sentence. Yet how could this be? Did not prisons observe and classify offenders and then send them to appropriate institutions to be reformed? True, overcrowding had made these things difficult, not enough prisoners were being reformed and therefore diverted from crime; but surely prisons were operating along the right lines, using the correct techniques? According to much official rhetoric this was the position, but in practice things were very different. Classification procedures involved little sophistication. In fact, they were very crude, while the military-style prison regime with its boring work routines – like sewing mailbags – did little to encourage reform by increasing personal responsibility. Against this it might be argued, and the Prison Commission took this line, that reconviction rates were reasonably good – that is, not too many offenders returned to prison to repeat the experience.

However, the simple fact that some offenders did not return to prison cannot be taken to mean that they were reformed by their prison experience, that they were persuaded in any positive way while serving their sentences to lead 'a good and useful life on discharge'. Interestingly, the White Paper endorsed this view, even going on to say that prisoners might be reformed 'in spite of' their training rather than because of it! This apparent lack of confidence in the potential of prisons as institutions capable of reform suggests an obvious contradiction. After all, the White Paper indicated a massive expansion of institutional provision, yet on the other hand was far from sanguine about their reforming potential, even allowing for the problems of overcrowding. How did Home Secretary Butler explain it?

Butler's position was that little was known about the causes of crime. Much more research was needed in this area, no less than in science and technology. Once this research was completed we would be in a better position to treat and cure the criminal; the human or social sciences were capable of providing us with the right tools. The terms 'treatment' or 'cure' were to be deliberately used. They suggested a pathological, quasi-scientific method whereby the 'diseased' individual offender would be fed into the institutional system, 'treated' or processed, and then returned to the community 'cured' or rehabilitated. This rehabilitative model, as it came to be called, was fundamentally different from old-fashioned reform. Whereas what the Prison Commission was still relying upon to achieve reform was not, in spite of its rhetoric, much more than an updated combination of Jeremy Bentham's desire to 'grind rogues honest' and John Howard's call for 'calm religious reflection', rehabilitation with its army of psychiatrists and psychotherapists was to have the benefit of science. Where hard work and God had failed, group therapy and Freud were to succeed. It was this promise that underpinned the Government's commitment to provide more institutions, even though their current efficacy was in doubt.

It is important to stress that this change of emphasis did not happen overnight in 1959. On the contrary, in a mid-1950s report on the progress of the prison system since the war, the Commissioners proudly announced that 'the sciences of psychiatry and psychology have been brought to bear on the mental care of inmates on a systematic basis. Three psychiatric clinics with a qualified medical staff, visiting psychotherapists, and psychiatric social workers have been set up for men and women'.[4] However, these provisions were modest and the White Paper agreed that 'much more remains to be done', pointing out that work would soon be starting on Britain's first purpose-built psychiatric prison at Grendon Underwood in Buckinghamshire. Home Secretary Butler may well have viewed the Prison Commission as being a little out of touch. The Commission had earlier avoided incorporation into the Home Office proper thanks to a Commons rebellion which overturned one of the provisions of the Criminal Justice Bill 1947, but it was living on borrowed time. Apart from its independence, being an administrative anachronism which belonged more to the nineteenth than the twentieth century, the sooner the Commission joined the Home Office alongside the centrally organised probation service with its growing commitment to psychiatrically-based casework the better it would be, particularly as probation officers would expect to have an increasing role in supervision of prisoners after release.

R. A. Butler's programme was skilfully sold to Parliament, and to the informed public. In the late 1950s it was progressive to be in favour of rehabilitation rather than reform, and it was a perspective which could, without too much difficulty, accommodate the rising demand for welfare rather than justice. Crucially, it could also accommodate the growing political consensus. In an increasingly prosperous society in which the Labour and Conservative parties were coming together, where it was widely believed that traditional class antagonisms were a thing of the past, it was far easier to believe that those who broke the social contract did so because they were maladjusted or ill and therefore in need of treatment, rather than because they were morally bad or somehow socially disaffected.

REFERENCES

1. *Prisons and Borstals* 4th edn, (HMSO: London, 1960) p. 57.
2. Ibid. p. 43.
3. P. HALL, H. LAND, R. PARKER and A. WEBB, *Change, Choice and Conflict in Social Policy*, Ch. 12, 'Detention Centres: the experiment which could not fail' (Heinemann: London, 1975) p. 344.
4. *Report of the Commissioners of Prisons for the Year 1954.* (HMSO: London) App. to Ch. 1 p. 17.

REHABILITATION AND WELFARE 1959–1970

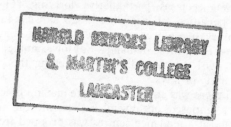

Labour's acceptance of rehabilitation in the late 1950s, like its growing commitment to abolish capital punishment, was part of a far wider process of Labour 'modernisation'. As the Party moved towards accepting the mixed economy, with Hugh Gaitskell's attack on Clause IV of Labour's constitution, so there was a restructuring of the Party's outlook at a moral level which was to have legislative consequences well into the 1960s with first, and predictably, the final abolition of capital punishment (1965), and later liberalising changes in the law in respect of homosexual behaviour (1967), abortion (1967) and divorce (1969). These efforts to make Britain a more humane and tolerant country to live in were not popular with all members of the Labour Party. There were, for example, many trade union MPs who felt that things were getting 'out of hand'. To an important extent then, as Stuart Hall rightly points out,[1] the Parliamentary majority for these changes had to be secured with the help of the progressive wing of the Conservative Party which in the postwar era had, in its turn, already played a crucial role in 'modernising' Conservative attitudes to the economy by both its advocacy of the Industrial Charter and full employment, and its continuing support for the Welfare State. However, the changes it secured at this level were far easier to sustain in the Party than social or moral reforms. So, for example, R. A. Butler's rehabilitative ideal, as well as the partial abolition of capital punishment (1957), were constantly attacked, particularly by rank and file Conservatives who at Party Conferences in the late 1950s and early 1960s generated a degree of vengeful rhetoric which startled even some of the popular dailies.

CHILDREN IN TROUBLE

The crime figures helped to buttress this fury. The number of indictable offences recorded by the police rose by 43 per cent between 1958 and 1962. The increase in recorded crimes by the young was seen as particularly worrying. The public wanted tougher penalties and not what it saw as weak-kneed welfare, and the Conservative Government went at least some of the way towards satisfying these demands. So, for example, the Criminal Justice Act 1961 was aimed at strengthening the penal system in a whole variety of ways.

First, there was an increase in the maximum level of fines which could be imposed on juveniles. Second, the minimum age for attendance at attendance centres was dropped from 12 to 10 while the number of hours required for attendance was increased. The Approved School system was also to be put right. No only was the Home Secretary given more powers to intervene in the management of these Schools, the temporary removal of unruly or subversive pupils was also authorised. It was intended that disturbances such as those that had happened at Carlton House would not be repeated. Finally, the Act reduced from 16 to 15 the minimum age at which Borstal training could be imposed.

These firm measures seemed justified to a government which had just come to terms with the rock-and-roll generation of the mid- and late 1950s; they seemed even more necessary when they were soon confronted by mods and rockers on the beaches at Brighton and Southend. Another moral panic was on the agenda. Needless to say, the Government's tough line in 1961 was not thought tough enough by some. There was, for example, a determined attempt during the second reading of the Criminal Justice Bill 1960 to reintroduce corporal punishment. Although this attempt was soundly beaten in the Commons, some fifty-seven Conservative MPs voted in favour of corporal punishment and against the Party Whip, no doubt arguing that their actions reflected public opinion which had been extensively polled on the subject in March 1960. It was partly anticipation of pressures like this that had persuaded the Home Secretary to refer the whole question of corporal punishment to the Advisory Council on the Treatment of Offenders (ACTO) two months earlier.

ACTO reported in favour of abolition. It found no conclusive proof that corporal punishment had been an especially effective deterrent before its abolition, or that its abolition had led to an increase in the offences for which it had previously been devised. The report also pointed out that before its abolition in 1948 corporal punishment had been available for only a very narrow range of offences. The present outcry seemed to envisage this range being considerably extended, yet to do this, argued the report, would 'mean putting the clock back not twelve years but a hundred years'. Facts like these, plus a skilful and deliberate focus on the mechanics of the punishment – men strapped to the triangle, held rigid by leather belts and collar – all helped to stem the tide against corporal punishment being reintroduced, though the issue was raised time and again in the 1960s.

There were other important skirmishes during the passage of the 1961 Act. For example, the proposal to merge the Prison Commission into the Home Office was again resisted, though the Government did finally succeed and the merger took place in 1963. There was also a row over detention centres. The proposal to open one for girls at Moor Court seemed pointless to some, there were hardly enough delinquent girls to warrant it. At a more general level Lord Longford, who was emerging strongly as a Labour spokesman on penal affairs, condemned the centres as negative and brutal. It was partly in an attempt to meet such criticisms that the Act included the new provision of aftercare for those leaving detention. At the same time aftercare was also made compulsory for certain other categories of offender. These provisions placed a significant new burden on the probation service which, following a recommendation from ACTO, was reorganised in the mid-1960s as the Probation and Aftercare Service. This restructuring of the service, combined with its expansion, caused anxieties, and these were added to by the controversy which surrounded the publication in 1965 of the Labour White Paper, *The Child, The Family and the Young Offender* (Cmnd 2742).

Labour's explanation of crime in the 1960s continued to focus on the 'acquisitive society'. There were, however, other Labour explanations on offer and these concerned the structure of the social services. The argument was that although the Conservatives had indeed under-financed the Welfare State, the real problem was not so much cash as organisation. The social services at local government level were divided between too many separate services; there was little co-ordination between them, and as a consequence some families fell through the welfare net altogether. It was from these 'problem families', as they came to be called, that so many juvenile delinquents came. If, therefore, local government social service departments could be reorganised to guarantee these families help then the growing problem of juvenile crime could be tackled at its roots. Coupled with this administrative reform, so typically Fabian in outlook, was Labour's contention that if children in trouble were more in need of welfare and support than simple justice and punishment then it might be as well to abolish juvenile courts. Laws of evidence and so on were quite unsuitable for dealing with young offenders, since very often the facts in such cases were not in dispute. A different setting was required, an informal family setting offering a wide range of flexible solutions. To achieve this Labour's White Paper on *The Child, the Family and the Young Offender* proposed to empower local authorities to appoint Family Councils made up of social workers and other suitably experienced people (op. cit., para. 12). These Councils would attempt to deal with each case as far as possible through negotiation with parents; only where no agreement could be reached would reference be made to a Family Court which would be made up of justices specially selected for their ability to deal with young people.

The idea that children and young people were in need of support, that those responsible for them should look more to their welfare than to justice or punishment to secure their future wellbeing and lawful behaviour, appealed strongly to those progressives whose rehabilitative ideal was far more concerned with the language of 'treatment' and 'cure' than old-fashioned justice and punishment. Indeed, to have argued for justice and punishment in the 1960s would have been thought to be very reactionary indeed. But argument there was; there was simply too much professional status at risk. The rival factions have been well defined by A. E. Bottoms[2]:

The main opposition came from lawyers, magistrates and probation officers. The last group is of particular interest, as they shared much of the psychoanalytic ideology of other social workers; but they also had a long tradition of independence of local authorities, and of service to courts, and it was from this standpoint that their critique was made. On the other side of the debate, the main supporters of the proposals were other social workers, particularly members of the child care service, and many of these talked openly of their gaining through the proposals much more professional prestige and recognition for their service which was still less than twenty years old.

The strength of the lobby against abolishing juvenile courts, and it included many Conservative MPs, and the sheer intensity of the justice versus welfare debate it provoked, caught the Labour Government by surprise and the White Paper with its strong welfare emphasis was never translated directly into practice. However, not to be deterred, Labour returned with fresh proposals in 1968. The new White Paper, *Children in Trouble* (Cmnd 3601) had a relatively easy passage, mainly because it retained juvenile courts. This concession apart, however, the new White Paper had much the same welfare emphasis as its predecessor. To achieve this a series of new proposals, most of which were written into the Children and Young Persons Act 1969, were put forward. These included a proposal that aimed to keep more children out of juvenile courts altogether by insisting on better liaison between the police and local authority children's departments to settle cases, wherever possible, on an informal basis. For those cases where this was not possible and the courts had to be involved, magistrates were to be given the power to issue a Care Order which placed the child in the care of the local authority, and it was for the social workers in that authority to decide where the child should be placed, say with a foster parent or in an institution. This was a restriction on magistrates' powers. They would no longer, for example, be able to directly order a child to be locked up in an institution; if that was to be done, it would be done solely on the authority of a social worker and not a magistrate. As for the institutions themselves, the White Paper proposed a large scale reorganisation. Approved Schools as such, and associated institutions like remand homes and reception centres, were to be abolished, or rather absorbed into a comprehensive new system of Community Homes.

The White Paper also pointed out that existing forms of treatment distinguished sharply between those that required removal from home and those that did not. Yet very often courts think something else is required, the power to enable children to stay at home and at the same time to come under the influence of a more constructive environment. If children before the courts could be advised or even ordered to take part in purposeful community activities – often with non-offenders – then this would surely help towards their rehabilitation. This was the thinking behind the case for a comprehensive range of Intermediate Treatment facilities to replace junior attendance centres which were thought to be inappropriate and would, in due course, be phased out.

Taken together all these provisions, translated into the 1969 Act, represented a second-round victory for welfare over justice. True, important changes concerning young offenders between 17 and 21 had been shelved and juvenile courts were retained at the expense of the proposed new Family Courts. On the other hand, nothing could disguise the welfare thrust of the new legislation with its emphasis on care rather than criminal proceedings. Equally firm, or so it seemed, were the limits imposed on magistrates to incarcerate the very young, while probation officers, traditional agents of the juvenile court, lost out to social workers in the professional struggle to supervise 'children in trouble'.

Not universally popular by any means, the 1969 Act came to be regarded by some of its Tory critics in much the same light as Labour's legislation on homosexuality and abortion, and its support for 'progressive' education; that is, as just another lurch in the direction of a permissive and morally irresponsible society. It is important to stress, however, that opposition to Labour's original White Paper came not only from Conservatives who felt that young offenders could only be deterred by tougher punishments. Of course there were Tories like Rhodes Boyson who took this view, arguing for a return to 'Victorian discipline' both in the home and at school. But there were also progressive Tories, particularly in Parliament, who could see the value of intervening to forestall delinquency. After all, it was a Conservative Government which went some way towards first allowing for this in the Childrens Act 1963. But what troubled even progressive Tories was Labour's conflation of welfare and justice. It might well be that welfare could forestall delinquency. But if it did not, and crimes were committed, then justice must take its course and that might not only involve punishment, but also due process, justice being seen to be done in a legally constituted court. This was no crude swipe at welfare, and as such, had little in common with the objections of the Tory Party's 'hang 'em and flog 'em' brigade.

THE WAR AGAINST CRIME

Labour's first set of proposals for young offenders had also been criticised in connection with the Royal Commission on the Penal System which was announced in the Conservative Government's White Paper, *The War Against Crime 1959–64* (Cmnd 2296). As this White Paper was partly intended as a straightforward report on changes since 1959, it is worth considering in some detail. It began by outlining the same strategy as its predecessor, *Penal Practice in a Changing Society*: that is, by arguing that the rising crime rate could best be dealt with by strengthening the police and making sure that the courts and the penal system were working as efficiently and as effectively as possible. The Government was clearly in a self-congratulatory mood over the police force, which since 1960 had increased in strength by about 10 per cent. As to the law and the courts, the Criminal Law Revision Committee was busily updating the law on larceny while the Streatfeild Committee's recommendations to ensure that courts have full information on offenders before sentence had already been brought into effect.

What about the penal system itself? How much progress had been made on that front? It will be recalled that in 1959 there was a feeling that perhaps the penal system had not been making its full contribution, that too many prisoners were getting little or no benefit from their prison or Borstal experience and were therefore returning to crime very soon after their release. One of the two reasons used to explain this disappointing performance was overcrowding. Penal institutions could reform, but not if their facilities were over-stretched, as they were, to the point where proper training was no longer possible. In 1959 then, the Government agreed to provide more penal institutions, and it is clear from *The War Against Crime* that the Conservative Government subsequently worked hard to meet that commitment. The increase, for example, in capital expenditure on prison service establishments from £822,000 in 1958/59 to £6,935,000 scheduled for 1964–65 shows just how much effort was being made. Between 1959 and 1964 the number of detention centres increased from four to fifteen. Five new Borstals were opened during the same period. There was also an increase in the accommodation available for adult prisoners; four new open prisons for men and one for women, plus the newly-built, ultra-modern secure prison for men at Blundeston. Apart from this expenditure on prison service establishments, the Government also committed more resources in other areas such as Approved Schools, where a budget of £15,000 in 1958–59 was increased to a proposed £2,250,000 for 1964–65.

So the list races on, more institutions, more money. Nor was it an expansion which could be halted since, although overcrowding had been relieved to some extent, conditions were still difficult, particularly in local prisons. Yet the outlook was perhaps a little brighter on this front, so some improvement in the prison service's capacity to turn offenders away from crime might be hoped for. Much would still depend though, as the 1959 White Paper had stressed, on devising successful rehabilitative regimes. What had been achieved since then? Were institutional regimes now progressing along the right lines? Had more research into the cause of crime and penal methods produced the hoped-for results?

The War Against Crime was cautious, suggesting that no one could answer 'Yes' to that question with complete assurance, and because of this uncertainty the Government had decided on a thorough stocktaking of the penal system as a whole, an inquiry by way of a Royal Commission into the purposes of the penal system and the methods by which these purposes were translated into practice. Members of the Commission were duly appointed in August 1964. Within eighteen months the Commission was disbanded. What had gone wrong?

There are a number of competing explanations, two of which concern the scope of the inquiry and the newly-elected Labour Government's determination to press ahead with its own initiatives. The terms of reference given to the Commission were indeed ambitious, perhaps too ambitious. It seems certain that several members of the Commission came to this conclusion and they subsequently resigned. Second, the Labour Government's White Papers on *The Adult Offender* (1965) and *The Child, The Family and the Young Offender* (1965) covered ground which was surely reserved for the Commission. Was further investigation really necessary? The Labour Government naturally tried to discount this view, which was how the Conservative Party saw things, concentrating more on the internal differences within the Commission about the scope and nature of its inquiry which had led to six resignations. Prime Minister Harold Wilson went so far as to imply that the Commission had virtually disbanded itself rather than become the victim of an impatient Labour Government, unwilling to listen to expert advice. As if to reinforce this interpretation it was announced that the Government's long-standing advisory body on the penal system, ACTO, which had been disbanded at the appointment of the Commission, was to be replaced by an expanded Advisory Council on the Penal System (1965).

Amid all this concern for the offender, there was a growing concern for the victims of crime, particularly among rank and file members of the Conservative Party. This showed itself most obviously in the Criminal Injuries Compensation Scheme, set up in 1964 to make *ex gratia* payment to people who had sustained personal injuries directly attributed to a crime of violence, or to an attempt to prevent a crime or make an arrest. Prior to 1964, victims of violent crimes could only seek compensation through the civil courts where success largely depended on the offenders being traced and convicted and, crucially, on their ability to pay. Although a change for the better, the new scheme had important limitations. For example, the injury had to be worth at least a claim of £150 or else it was simply not considered, while the scheme did not apply at all in cases of domestic violence. Finally, the scheme received very little publicity in the 1960s and therefore many victims who might have benefited from its provisions were not even aware of its existence. Obviously much more still needed to be done on this front, but as things turned out compensation to victims of violence very quickly slipped out of the Government's list of priorities when faced with what it interpreted as an increasingly unstable prison system.

PRISON REGIMES AND PRISON SECURITY

In 1963 allegations were made by an ex-prisoner about ill-treatment in Durham prison. An inquiry by the prison's Visiting Committee did not uphold the allegations, though in one case it was inclined to believe that a prisoner had been beaten, even though this could not be decisively proved. This incident apart, the inquiry spoke in most glowing terms about the prison, which is surprising to say the least, since Durham was gaining an unenviable reputation as one of the toughest prisons in the country, especially the regime in its special wing. To cope with what it took to be a new breed of 'violent and dangerous' criminals the Prison Commission had devised special wings in one or two secure prisons. Conditions in these wings were meant to be tough, they were places where 'prisoners were broken'. (For a personal account see *McVicar by Himself*.)[3] The special wing at Durham was made even more oppressive in 1965 when it was modified for the arrival of the three Great Train Robbers, Goody, Field and James. Electronic surveillance and armed guards were among the new security measures introduced. Things got even worse after Ronald Biggs escaped from Wandsworth. At one point troops were called in and Durham's Chief Constable even went so far as to suggest that limited nuclear weapons might be used to free the Train Robbers – 'Nothing is too extravagant'!

Public anxiety over prison security was fuelled a year later by the escape of the spy George Blake and a prisoner, Frank Mitchell, whom the press dubbed the 'mad axeman of Dartmoor'. Finding himself under some political pressure, Home Secretary Jenkins announced that Lord Mountbatten would head an inquiry 'into recent prison escapes, with particular reference to that of George Blake, and to make recommendations for the improvement of prison security'. Mountbatten's Report included the sharp observation that conditions in various special wings were 'as such no country with a record for civilised behaviour ought to tolerate any longer than is absolutely necessary as a stop-gap measure'. What Mountbatten recommended for the long term was a single purpose-built high security prison which would take all those prisoners at present in the security wings, and more. To facilitate prison security in general the Report suggested a four-fold classification of prisoners, from category 'A' to category 'D', according to their security risk and the danger their escape might bring to the public and the police. The Government accepted this recommendation and about 140 prisoners were classified as category 'A'. It was prisoners from this category who were housed in the special wings. Other recommendations to improve the overall security of prison buildings, especially at the perimeter, were accepted and the Labour Government spent £2.5 million on searchlights, electronic scanning equipment, two-way radios and so on.

Where the Government hesitated was over Mountbatten's call for an Alcatraz-type prison, eventually opting instead for a policy of dispersal. That is, category 'A' prisoners – which included many 'lifers' after the abolition of the death penalty – were dispersed among three or four long-term prisons whose security had been upgraded. Segregation units were also provided in these prisons for particularly troublesome prisoners. The Prison Officers Association strongly opposed the dispersal policy and continued to call for a single prison to house all the 'hard cases'.

Attempts to put the prison system on a better footing, to make its rehabilitative ideal a reality, were genuinely made. Apart from more buildings, a call in *The Lancet*[4] for an official enquiry into the future of the prison medical service was swiftly answered by the Home Secretary who appointed a working party which concluded that the prison medical service should be expanded, that it was not undertaking enough research and that in particular it was not employing enough doctors with psychiatric training. A survey carried out for the working party showed that of the 140 doctors in the prison medical service, only 11 had the Diploma in Psychiatric Medicine. Further, although no specific recommendation was made to incorporate the prison medical service into the National Health Service – prison doctors were strongly opposed to this – the working party did recommend more secondments from the prison medical service to the NHS, and also argued for joint prison service/ NHS appointments whereby psychiatrists would be expected to divide their working week between the prison and outside NHS clinics. This was a modest attempt to break down the insularity of the prison medical service, and by 1967 three joint appointments had been made. Apart from the 'science' of psychiatry, psychology was also increasingly represented. By 1967 there were over 30 full-time psychologists in post and they were employed not only in testing and classification but also in group therapy and advising the management on prison routines. Needless to say, this expansion was seen as progressive, yet another step towards achieving the rehabilitative ideal. This at least was the official view.

The 1960s saw important developments in the organisation of the penal system for women. Ruth Ellis, whose execution in 1955 had left such an indelible mark on the public conscience, was hanged in Holloway, the same gaunt north London prison where suffragettes had been force-fed before 1914. In December 1968 Callaghan announced that Holloway was to be rebuilt. It would eventually provide nationwide facilities, including psychiatric and medical services. In short it was to be developed as a secure hospital. This pattern of treatment faithfully reflects official ideas about the female offender, the belief that women who commit crime are somehow psychologically or medically ill or unstable. Perceptions of the female offender provided the ideal vehicle for the new language of rehabilitation. Although there was some increase in the number of women and girls held in custody towards the end of the 1960s, the size of the female prison population has always been relatively small when compared to that of men, and since the war until the mid-1970s fairly stable, at between 800 and 1,000. The regime for both women and girls tended to mirror traditional ideas about the female's social role as mother and housekeeper, with perhaps some unskilled industrial work thrown in to confirm their place at the lower end of the dual labour market.

Callaghan had been preceded as Home Secretary by Roy Jenkins, who shortly before leaving the Home Office had taken responsibility for introducing a new Criminal Justice Bill (1966). The provisions of this Bill were to give legal status to the policies outlined in Labour's White Paper, *The Adult Offender* (1965). Corrective training and preventive detention were duly abolished, and a new form of extended sentence was introduced to replace them. Next came the provision for parole or early release which was to be determined largely by the prisoner's response to training, how far he was along the road to rehabilitation. The idea was that there is a recognisable peak in the rehabilitative process after which prisoners are likely to deteriorate unless released. Briefly, while separate arrangements were made for lifers, parole was to be available to prisoners serving determinate sentences of over eighteen months. The procedure was for a prisoner to make his application for parole to a Local Review Committee which would built up a dossier on the prisoner containing reports about his progress in prison, recent home circumstances and so on. Once the Committee had come to its decision, this was passed on to the Parole Board which had the final say. There was no provision for a Parole Board in the original 1966 Bill. Roy Jenkins wanted the final decision on parole to rest with the Home Secretary. There was, however, a strong feeling in Parliament that a more broadly-based Parole Board composed of people with relevant experience would do a better job than most Home Secretaries and, under pressure, Jenkins reluctantly conceded. Finally, prison conditions were also affected by the Bill's provision for the suspended sentence. In future Courts were to be allowed to suspend a sentence – in some cases it was mandatory to do so – for a given period, and providing the offender did not get into trouble again during that period, the sentence would lapse, it would be considered spent. If, on the other hand, he did re-offend during the specified period, then the original sentence would be reactivated and an additional punishment handed out to cover the new offence.

Parole, like the suspended sentence, was designed to reduce the number of people in prison. The Home Secretary estimated that once the scheme got underway at least 20 per cent of those entitled to parole would benefit from it, thus making for a reduction in the average daily prison population of around 600. True, the Parole Board's initial caution meant that in the first year only 8.5 per cent of those eligible for parole were released, but the impact of parole taken together with the suspended sentence did help to keep prison numbers down, initially at least. The crucial question was, would this improvement last?

The control of category 'A' prisoners continued to be a problem. The Prison Department seemed either unwilling or unable to provide these prisoners with anything like a positive regime. The riot at Parkhurst prison in October 1969 showed the full extent of the Department's failure. Parkhurst had been simmering for some time. Out of a prison population of around 350, 50 were regularly category 'A' prisoners. The dangers inherent in this policy of concentration were intensified by the tightening up of prison security following the Mountbatten Report. Parkhurst, like most other prisons, had its share of more barbed wire, more patrols and so on. In addition activities like football matches or working prison allotments were cancelled. It was in protest against these restrictions, and also against the brutality of some prison officers, that 120 prisoners signed a public complaint. Callaghan acted swiftly, appointing a member of the prison service to conduct an internal inquiry. The Gale Report, as it came to be known, was ready in June 1969 but never published. Apart from Callaghan's known antipathy towards open government, were there any other reasons why the Report was held back? The general view seems to be that although the Report concluded that the prisoners' complaints had some basis in fact, they would nonetheless be difficult to prove. In the circumstances, Callaghan obviously decided to sweep what dirt there was under the carpet, only recommending a few staffing changes to give the appearance that something was really being done. The futility of this low-key approach in the face of such a potentially dangerous situation was amply demonstrated just four months later when Parkhurst erupted into the worst prison riot since the Dartmoor mutiny in 1932. Twenty-eight prisoners and 35 officers were injured, and in the subsequent trial the alleged ringleaders were sentenced to additional terms of imprisonment of up to six years.

The Government's miscalculation is difficult to defend. Apart from the particular circumstances of Parkhurst, there was plenty of evidence from elsewhere in the system to show that prison regimes had toughened – up to breaking-point. Two years earlier, for example, there had been the first of two serious disturbances at Durham. With incidents like these still warm in his file it is hard to understand why Callaghan was so slow to recognise the stormclouds gathering over Parkhurst.

CAPITAL PUNISHMENT: ABOLITION

The abolition of the death penalty, which contributed to the problems of prison security, had taken place in 1965, eight years after the Conservative Government's Act to limit the penalty by drawing a distinction between capital and non-capital murders. The intervening years were to demonstrate just how unsatisfactory such a distinction was, and abolition groups began to wonder what had really been achieved in 1957. Take, for example, the case of Harris, who was hanged for his part in a murderous assault by a group of four young men, even though he never actually struck a blow – all he had done was to search the hapless victim. The parallel between this case and the Craig/Bentley affair was close enough to galvanise the National Campaign for the Abolition of the Death Penalty into renewed activity in 1960. Widespread public disquiet over the operation of the 1957 Act was reflected in April of the following year when thousands attended an Albert Hall meeting which raised over £2,000 for the National Campaign. The work of the Campaign seemed even more urgent with the controversial conviction of James Hanratty for the 'A6 murder' early in 1962. Many people felt at the time that an innocent man had been hanged, that Hanratty was the victim of mistaken identity.

The election of a Labour Government in 1964 was taken to be a good omen by the abolitionists, and this optimism was justified. Harold Wilson favoured airing the question again and pledged that the Government would find the necessary time for a Private Member's Bill to be debated and the outcome to be decided by a free vote. By December 1964 Silverman's Murder (Abolition of the Death Penalty) Bill was before the Commons for its crucial second reading. It was easily passed, by 355 votes to 170. This was a far larger Commons majority than in the past, and is mostly explained by growing support for abolition in the Conservative Party in Parliament. There were, however, determined attempts to modify the Bill. These mainly centred on the case for exceptions, that is, abolition was acceptable in principle but for certain murders, say of a policeman in pursuit of his duty, or a prison warder, the death penalty should be retained. All these amendments were defeated. What did succeed, though, was an amendment to abolish the death penalty for a trial period of five years only, after which the whole question would have to be considered again by Parliament. To many members, in both parties, this seemed a sensible precaution and it was with this amendment that the Bill was sent to the Lords.

Surprisingly, perhaps, there was little sustained opposition in the Lords, though one important amendment allowed judges to recommend a minimum for those murderers sentenced to 'life' imprisonment. The clergy had changed their tune, and in a tactful speech Lord Chief Justice Parker argued that he was in favour of abolition because he found the 1957 Act unworkable. The Bill was passed without difficulty, by 204 votes to 104 on its second reading. This represents a dramatic shift in opinion over the years. In 1948 the Lords could only muster 28 votes for abolition, in 1956, 95. What had caused this change? Were the Lords simply reflecting a significant shift in public opinion on this issue? There is no evidence for this. Public opinion polls still showed a decisive majority for retaining the death penalty, at least in some form. Perhaps the Lords simply changed their minds because once having learned to live with legislation which limited the death penalty, abolition no longer seemed such a great step, particularly as the provision was to be reviewed after five years. A less generous but equally plausible explanation is that the Lords feared what a future Labour Government might do to them if they 'misbehaved' by throwing out a Bill which had such a decisive Commons majority on a free vote.

The abolition of the death penalty had a certain bizarre consequence for Sidney Silverman. As the MP most identified with abolition he was opposed in Nelson and Colne by a pro-hanging candidate in the 1966 general election. Patrick Downey was no ordinary candidate. He was uncle to Lesley Ann Downey, a victim of the moors murderers Ian Brady and Myra Hindley, whose cruel acts had so enraged public opinion and made more than one abolitionist waver. As things turned out, Silverman won easily. His support for abolition stretched back over many years, it was well known to his constituents in Nelson and Colne, and it was always unlikely that they would wait until now to reject him. However, Patrick Downey received over 5,000 votes and the media attention he attracted helped to give the impression that the issue was far from settled. At a parliamentary level, Duncan Sandys MP, in response to public concern at the killing of three policemen in Shepherds Bush in 1966, kept the pressure on by seeking leave to introduce a Bill to restore the death penalty for the murder of policemen. Although defeated, Sandys' initiative attracted 170 votes; it was perhaps the sort of compromise which appealed to those ambivalent members whose constituency parties were still baying for blood. This was particularly true for the Conservative Party whose rank and file members behaved as if abolition symbolised the 'permissive society' which they felt, quite rightly, was being legislated for above their heads. Some resentment was directed at those Party managers who it was believed actually connived to keep capital punishment off the Party Annual Conference agenda. In fact, pressure for the issue to be raised was too great to be ignored altogether and amendments calling for the reintroduction of capital punishment in one form or another were debated on Law and Order motions at Conference in 1966 and again in 1969.

The statutory provision for abolition was due to expire in July 1970, unless Parliament voted otherwise. This put Home Secretary Callaghan in a difficult position since the vote might well coincide with the run-up to a general election. To avoid this, Callaghan brought the issue forward to December 1969, six months before the end of the officially defined experimental period. This not unreasonably annoyed the pro-hanging lobby, and the Conservative Opposition was persuaded to put forward an official motion of censure. This was defeated, the debate duly took place, and the issue was decided in favour of continuing with abolition. Some mention was made of statistics from the *Murder 1957–1968* report which had just been published by the Home Office, but these figures were far from conclusive, in either direction, and the issue was decided, as it always had been, more on first principles than statistics. The figures showed that there had been little shift in the balance of opinion in Parliament since 1965.

REHABILITATION AS MYTH

If the penal lobby was, for the most part anyway, delighted about abolition, it was far from happy about the prison system itself. The disturbances at Durham and Parkhurst were difficult to explain in the sense that the 1960s were supposed to have been the decade when all prisoners were to be 'cured' of their criminality and re-turned, with the help of the psychiatrist and psychologist, to the community as law-abiding citizens. Was the rhetoric of rehabili-tation turning out like the rhetoric of old-fashioned reform, a simple ideological construct which bore no relation to what was going on in practice, a mere progressive language which enabled the Prison Department to obscure what was really happening inside our pris-ons? The short answer must be Yes.

But how did it happen, what blunted the promise of the rehabili-tative ideal? One explanation is that it was never really given a chance, that the Mountbatten recommendations which emphasised security were implemented at the expense of treatment. If this is the case then a large share of the blame must fall on Roy Jenkins. It was his decision to extend the inquiry into George Blake's escape to the prison system as a whole. He had no need to do this, the in-quiry could have been confined to the spy Blake alone. So why did Jenkins widen the inquiry's terms of reference? Richard Crossman probably offered the best explanation, arguing that the Conserva-tive Party were hoping to make another 'security scandal' out of Blake's escape by linking it to the Russians. Roy Jenkins, anxious to avoid fishing in such treacherous political waters, sought to de-flect public attention away from Blake's case in particular by locat-ing it in the more general problem of security throughout the entire prison system. It was a neat political manoeuvre, but it undoubted-ly led to a disastrous toughening-up of the prison system and cer-tainly many informed sources, like the Howard League, were to claim that it was playing havoc with the rehabilitative ideal. The

Mountbatten Report, it seems, became the whipping boy, the main cause of treatment's failure. But this is hardly convincing since even if 'treatment' did work, even if, that is, the rehabilitative ideal was achievable, there is no evidence that it was in full stride before Mountbatten, only to be crushed towards the end of the 1960s. On the contrary, the evidence we have already considered about the level of prison psychiatric and related services indicates plainly enough that the surface had only been scratched. What could a handful of psychiatrists and psychologists do in a prison population of over 30,000? Very little, and although Mountbatten may have slowed up what progress there had been, its impact was hardly decisive.

Arguably more important was the hostile way in which the new 'sciences' were regarded by ordinary prison medical officers. Many of them felt capable of dealing with those in their charge without the interference of 'new-fangled' medicine, and as a consequence the joint NHS/prison service appointments never worked well. Psychiatric reports to the courts may have improved but that was about the full extent of any progress. Treatment was pretty minimal, how could it be otherwise in so hostile an environment? And no one, it should be stressed, was more hostile than the basic grade of prison officer. Old-fashioned reform, in theory at least, had given him a role. True, not many officers really believed in reform – and in this they were less naive than their employers – but it did at least offer those who did the chance to view their job in a constructive light, while at the same time enabling their union to argue for more cash on the grounds that its members were more than 'mere turn-keys'. The rehabilitative ideal put all this into jeopardy. The prison welfare officer, now a seconded probation officer trained in the casework approach, was to team up with a growing number of prison psychiatrists and psychologists and together they were now to be charged with 'curing' the prisoner, or persuading him to turn away from crime and lead a good and useful life on release. This was the scenario – in fact, as we have seen, far too positive by half – which the prison officers envisaged, and it represented a direct threat to what little status they had so far achieved. This professional concern, combined with the honest belief that the 'mumbo-jumbo' of psychiatry was nonsense, fuelled their opposition to 'treatment' and the new post-Mountbatten emphasis on security was welcomed with relish. This enthusiasm for tightening-up had some public support. In the so-called permissive 1960s which had begun with mods and rockers at Southend and Brighton and, if the media are to be believed, ended with long-haired drug-taking hippies 'just about everywhere', there were plenty of people, Labour voters as well as Conservatives, who thought things had gone 'too far', that even prisoners were idling their time away watching TV instead of being 'made to suffer' for their crimes. However, it is important to re-state the point that although the prison officers' response to Mount-batten may have been tough, some would say brutal, it can hardly have led to the collapse of the 'treatment' regime; that regime was something which still existed more in the collective mind of the Prison Department than in operational reality.

As we have seen, there was too, in the 1960s, much talk of wel-fare. Young offenders, in particular, had to be seen as people more in need of welfare and support than simple justice and punishment. Three things have to be remembered about all this talk. In the first place, legislation to incorporate this new emphasis was resisted, it was not until the decade had virtually passed that it reached the stat-ute book. Second, the period in question saw a huge increase in the number of institutions available for 'dealing with' young of-fenders, particularly hard-line institutions like detention centres. Third, and to anticipate, important provisions in the Children and Young Persons Act 1969 were never translated into practice, and the welfare promise of Labour's legislation was never properly ful-filled. The welfare progressives had little to show for all their effort.

The apparent, if slow, collapse of the rehabilitative ideal led many people away from the idea that criminals are ill, that they could somehow be taken into institutions and cured. Perhaps ex-planations of crime and criminal behaviour lay more in society than in individual pathology. And who knows, the offender might turn out to be rational too! The investment in institutions which had been so proudly announced in 1959, and which subsequent Labour and Conservative governments had fought hard to honour, was seen as questionable, as was the justice of holding offenders in these in-stitutions until it was judged, fairly arbitrarily, that they had been somehow 'cured'. It was in response to these ideas, as well as the wish to spread and develop them, that Radical Alternatives to Pris-on (RAP) was founded in 1970, the same year as the Government's own Advisory Council published what was to be a highly influential report on non-custodial and semi-custodial penalties, the Wootton Report. The search for justice and alternatives was about to begin in earnest, and in a climate which was far from the heady political consensus of the Swinging Sixties.

REFERENCES

1. NATIONAL DEVIANCY CONFERENCE (ed.), *Permissiveness and Social Control* (Macmillan: London, 1980).
2. R. HOOD (ed.) *Crime, Criminology and Public Policy* (Heinemann: London, 1974) pp. 329–30.
3. JOHN MCVICAR, *McVicar by Himself* (Arrow: London, 1979).
4. *The Lancet*, 7 Oct. 1961.

Chapter three

JUSTICE AND ALTERNATIVES 1970–1982

The prosperity which many people enjoyed in the late 1950s and throughout the 1960s could not hide Britain's relative economic decline. Compared with key competitors like Germany and France our industrial performance was far from strong, and it was to get worse throughout the 1970s. The strain of this decline, and the measures taken to counteract it, such as legal curbs on trade union power, soon led to serious industrial conflict and the breakup of the political consensus. So, by the end of the 1970s the Conservative Party's lurch to the right in favour of monetarism was challenged by what many members of the Labour Party came to see as their own genuinely socialist response, the Alternative Economic Strategy. At a moral level too, there were attempts to deconstruct the consensus. Individual moral entrepreneurs like Mary Whitehouse and Malcolm Muggeridge joined in eagerly with organised pressure groups like the Festival of Light in an attempt to mobilise the 'silent majority' against the permissive society. Not surprisingly, this put pressure on the parliamentary coalition which had legislated for the so-called permissive society and there were, for example, determined attempts in Parliament during the 1970s to reintroduce capital punishment and tighten up the law on abortion.

The mainstream of the penal system was also affected by this moral backlash. The rehabilitative ideal, the notion that many offenders are unanswerable for their actions but ill and in need of treatment was directly at odds with the new emphasis on personal moral responsibility which held that offenders should be made accountable for their crimes and punished accordingly. The demonstrable failure of penal institutions to effect rehabilitation lent support to this 'new' and increasingly tough approach. So too, ironically perhaps, did those sociological perspectives on deviancy which in the late 1960s and early 1970s sought to demystify the deviant, to portray him as a rational man who made rational choices, neither a victim of his environment nor somehow diseased. Indeed, he is much like the rest of us and even if his punishment is to be severe, say imprisonment, this is not sufficient reason to deny him those basic human rights which we would readily accord to other 'ordinary' men. Just how little the Home Office cared for this line of reasoning was shown by its response to the prison demonstrations of 1972.

PRISONERS' RIGHTS

In the year following the introduction of parole and the suspended sentence there was a noticeable drop in the prison population, from 35,009 in 1967 to 32,461 in 1968. This improvement, however, was shortlived. By 1970 the prison population was again on the increase, and was already well past the figure for 1967. What to do about our overcrowded prisons became one of the central issues in penal policy during the 1970s. Of particular concern was the growing number of prisoners held on remand pending trial. Conditions for these prisoners, even though many would later receive only non-custodial sentences, were truly appalling, worse in many ways than the conditions inflicted on convicted prisoners. Some form of trouble seemed inevitable, and it came early in 1972 with disturbances at Brixton prison where conditions were known to be especially bad.

It was at the time of these disturbances that a union for the Preservation of the Rights of Prisoners (PROP) was formed by a small group of ex-prisoners who drew up a 'Prisoners' Charter of Rights' which demanded, among other things: the right to trade union membership and the right to negotiate pay and conditions with the Home Office; the right to institute legal proceedings of any kind without first securing the consent of the Home Office; the right to consult legal advisers in confidence without interference, intervention or censorship by the prison authorities; the right to be legally represented and to call defence witnesses at internal disciplinary hearings; the right to parole according to well-established and known criteria; the right to a reasoned judgement on the Parole Board's decision and the right to challenge that decision in the courts; the right to communicate freely with the press and public; the right to receive and send as many letters as required without censorship; the right to consult an independent medical adviser.

These far-reaching demands echoed throughout the prison system, and by August 1972 PROP felt confident enough to organise a sit-down demonstration to publicise its Charter. This involved between 5,000 and 10,000 prisoners. Given that PROP's links with those on the inside were haphazard, this level of support was impressive, and showed just how tense the prison scene had become. Although prepared to admit that prison conditions were deteriorating, the Home Office refused to negotiate directly with PROP. Indeed, it seemed to adopt the view that the very idea of a union for the rights of prisoners was somehow preposterous. This was an attitude shared by some members of the public who began to ask, 'Who do these people think they are? What claims can prisoners possibly have to rights, surely by their criminal actions they have forfeited any such claims?'

A direct result of the prison disturbances was the introduction of control units. Speaking at his Association's annual conference in May 1973, the chairman of the Prison Officers Association (POA) claimed that most of the prison disturbances since 1968 had been caused by 'dangerous psychopaths'. If these people could be isolated from the mainstream of the prison system then future trouble could be avoided. This was, in effect, a renewed call for the implementation of the Mountbatten Report's recommendation for the construction of a special maximum security prison to house all category 'A' prisoners. This demand was rejected by the Home Secretary, Robert Carr. He felt that such a prison would be a sure recipe for disaster. Prisoners sent there would feel that they had reached the 'end of the line', that they had 'nothing to lose'. Who could guarantee discipline in a hopeless situation like that? But the Home Secretary did at least agree with the POA that there was an identifiable nucleus of 'trouble-makers' who had to be dealt with, and to this end he announced the setting up of two control units. Exactly how these would differ from segregation units where the regime was tough already was not made clear. All Home Secretary Carr would say was that prisoners allocated to these units might stay there for long periods of time.

Nothing else was known about these units until *The Sunday Times* broke the news about Michael Williams, one of the first prisoners to be allocated to the units. Williams was apparently in 'a bad way', and this was hardly surprising given what was happening to him, details of which were eventually prised out of the Home Office. Briefly, the control unit regime was divided into two phases, each normally lasting for an expected minimum period of ninety days. During the first phase the emphasis was on isolation from other prisoners. Any work done, educational or leisure activities, had to be carried out in the prisoner's cell. He was isolated for twenty-three hours in every day. For the remaining hour he was allowed to exercise and worship with other prisoners. Even contact with prison officers was deliberately kept to a minimum and if the prisoner misbehaved, say argued with a prison officer, he reverted to day one. The second phase allowed for a measure of activity with other prisoners, the purpose of which was purely functional, allowing the authorities to gauge whether he had 'learnt his lesson', whether he was prepared to co-operate instead of 'bucking the system'.

Public disquiet about this arbitrary and harsh system gathered momentum throughout 1974 and 1975, and eventually the Government gave in. At first there were minor concessions about how the regime was operated, but then in October 1975 the Home Secretary, Roy Jenkins, who had inherited the control units from his Conservative predecessor, announced that the whole regime was to be phased out. The units themselves, however, were not to be dismantled as such, but reserved for those prisoners who had to be removed from the rest of the prison population 'in the interests of good order and discipline'. Not surprisingly, perhaps, this announcement left some groups in the penal lobby wondering whether they had simply won a battle but lost the war. Discipline through segregation was still officially favoured and who could be sure what this might mean in the future?

ALTERNATIVES TO CUSTODY

The continuing pressure on the prison system had already forced the Government to step up its search for more alternatives to custody, and several new non-custodial sentences were introduced in the Criminal Justice Act 1972. The most important of these was the provision for community service, which had been recommended by ACPS in its 1970 report on non-custodial and semi-custodial penalties. What this provided for was that someone convicted of an offence normally punishable by imprisonment might instead be asked to do community service work at the discretion of a probation officer who would arrange for him to be attached to some local project. Offenders who would normally have been imprisoned were to be out in the community building adventure playgrounds, helping the handicapped and generally making themselves useful.

It has been argued that the rapid acceptance of community service by the courts owes much to the probation service which lost no time in learning how to 'manage' placements. There is some truth in this. However, there was some resistance from probation officers, which is perhaps hardly surprising. After all, for some years (as we have already seen) the offenders had more often than not been thought of as emotionally or mentally disturbed, even ill and therefore in need of a cure. This had led to the professionalisation of the various treatment services; the prison service with psychiatrists and psychologists, the probation officer trained with a psychoanalytical bias to be used in one-to-one casework situations, and so on. Obviously, not all probation officers took kindly to the idea that the criminal could now be 'treated', or changed for the better as the ACPS hoped, simply by 'mucking in' under the 'wholesome influence' of other community volunteers. The extent of the probation service's changing role can be gauged by the fact that in the ten years after 1966 the Crown Court's use of probation orders dropped by around 50 per cent.

Another alternative, the Newham Alternatives Project set up by RAP in 1974, also owed its origin to the Criminal Justice Act 1972 which introduced the deferred sentence. This allowed judges to defer passing sentence on an offender in order to take into account some expected change in his circumstances which might reasonably set him on the right road. For example, a convicted offender might plead that he had a new job lined up and that this would make all the difference to his prospects. In simple terms what the Newham Alternatives Project hoped to be was a key factor in those changed circumstances, a centre where offenders on deferred sentence could go for support and advice in an attempt to 'pull things together' and avoid the downward spiral to prison.

Other alternatives to prison were developed around this time by government-sponsored organisations like the National Association for the Care and Re-settlement of Offenders (NACRO). Set up in 1966 as part of the radical reorganisation of aftercare, NACRO soon moved into the business of demonstration projects, that is, projects which were aimed not simply at providing basic aftercare but which were intended to show that for many offenders prison is unnecessary. The New Careers project which was started at Bristol in 1972 illustrates this strategy. NACRO persuaded local judges, with Home Office support, to allow them to operate a scheme whereby selected young offenders could be trained to work in welfare agencies, youth clubs, community centres and the like instead of being sent to Borstal. The young offenders lived in a hostel as a condition of their probation and undertook a twelve-month training programme. For those who completed the programme successfully help was given to find permanent work in a social or welfare agency. NACRO also initiated the Hammersmith Teenage Project which was a non-residential scheme for youngsters between 12 and 16 who had been in trouble with the law or were thought to be in danger of committing crime. Those referred were assigned to 'link workers' who made contact with the youngster's family and generally helped those in their charge to 'cope with their environment'.

It is important to stress that there was much more to this mushrooming of alternatives than a simple wish to reduce the pressure on the prison system. True, by the mid-1970s thousands of prisoners were regularly having to share a cell, so anything which helped to relieve this pressure would be welcomed. However, for many people running alternative projects this was only half the story. That is, the decline of the treatment model, the belief that crime could be explained in terms of individual pathology, was replaced by the understanding that crime and criminal behaviour is better understood in wider social terms. It was a short step, but by no means a logical one, from this position to the idea that if offenders were to be 'rehabilitated' at all then it was much more likely to happen in society, in the community. Community 'treatment' then, became progressive and attempts to measure the success rate of alternative projects against the known failure of prison were soon to become standard practice.

At an ideological level this development was necessary since many of the important alternatives we have referred to did not get fully underway until the mid-1970s. By that time a law-and-order 'crisis' was firmly on the political agenda. Talk about consensus and harmony was replaced by talk which suggested that our inner cities were ghettos of fear and violence, that Britain was becoming ungovernable in the face of extra-parliamentary opposition to duly elected governments, as with the miners' industrial action in 1973–74. All these fears were exploited by the new Conservative Leader Margaret Thatcher whom many rank and file Conservatives rightly saw as their natural ally not only against the political consensus, but also against the by now faltering 'moral consensus' which had been constructed against their wishes, and which had always been 'soft on crime'. In this sometimes hysterical climate, arguments for 'soft' alternatives to prison needed all the supporting evidence they could get. (For more on law and order see Part Two.)

Apart from providing alternatives, the Criminal Justice Act 1972 also hoped to reduce the prison population by other means, including a revision of the suspended sentence. As we have already seen (Ch. 2), the suspended sentence was introduced in two forms, required or mandatory in certain circumstances, discretionary in others. It was the mandatory provision which was now to be withdrawn. Prisons were overcrowded with offenders on short sentences and the mandatory suspension of such sentences, except in some cases, was a bold stroke by the then Labour Government to remove these offenders from the system altogether, and so help to reduce the overall prison population. For a number of reasons, including the fact that many offenders were reconvicted of further offences during their period of supervision and therefore received further sentences in addition to those originally imposed, the expected benefits from this new sentence did not materialise. Indeed, many argued that it eventually led to an *increase* in the prison population, the exact opposite of its intention. The 1972 Act also made provision for changes in parole. Local Review Committees were to get more autonomy, they would no longer have to submit their every decision to be vetted by the central Parole Board.

This attempt to streamline the parole decision-making process was widely welcomed. Waiting for the outcome of a parole application is a tense business. The sooner prisoners know what the decision is, the better. However, it has to be said that by the mid-1970s parole was criticised on a number of fronts; its slowness was the least of its problems. For example, there was the vexed question of the Board's refusal to give reasons for its decisions, even if parole was refused. To get a 'knock-back' from the Board is difficult for prisoners to take in itself, to be refused reasons makes the disappointment even worse. How can a prisoner work for a favourable result the next time if he is not told why he failed previously? To many people this seemed to go against the principles of natural justice, and throughout the 1970s there was a growing demand that reasons should be given. Of course the factors involved – home circumstances, for example – touch on sensitive issues for the prisoner, but then so do those decisions made by Mental Health Tribunals, yet they have a provision for giving reasons if a case is turned down. More fundamentally, perhaps, the whole rationale of parole was called into question by an attack on its principal assumption, namely that it is possible to identify the point at which prisoners reach a peak in their training or treatment, when they are, as it were, on the road to rehabilitation. Once the belief got around that prisons did not change offenders for the better, that the whole rehabilitative paradigm was little more than an ideological construct, then parole became a natural target. The Board, it was argued, could no more tell when prisoners had 'peaked in their training' than they could predict who would most likely re-offend on release. This trenchant criticism led in one direction: parole should be abolished and replaced by a system of automatic release, say after a third of a sentence. Allied to this abolitionist perspective was a growing distrust of executive discretion. The argument became that it was for the courts to decide on the length of a prisoner's sentence and not the executive; and certainly not an executive which used frankly unjust procedures as in parole, where the prisoner was given no reasons for a refusal, where he could not attend his own hearing or be legally represented, and where he could not appeal. This was executive discretion of the worst and most arbitrary kind, and so to trust in justice rather than rehabilitation was now progressive.

TOUGHER STILL FOR THE YOUNG

Anxiety over executive discretion also led to a very bad press for the ACPS Report on young adult offenders (17–21) in 1974. The Council decided that there was little to choose between Borstal, detention centre and prison sentences. It therefore recommended that they should be replaced by a single sentence, the custody and control order. This order was to provide for a period spent in custody in a local 'neighbourhood' institution – to replace detention centres, Borstals and prisons for young offenders – followed by a period of supervision in the community by the probation service. The timing of the offender's transfer from custody to supervision would be decided on the advice of a local licence advisory committee. Opposition to this procedure was strong. It resembled parole, and was therefore rejected by a growing number of people who felt that sentences should be awarded on the basis of the seriousness of the offence committed and then left alone, untampered with by the executive on the basis of some correctional fantasy.

The controversy over the Council's Report forced the Labour Government into a long delay, and 'dealing with' young offenders was eventually left to the Conservatives, elected into office on a strong law-and-order ticket in 1979. The new Government was not convinced that the regimes in Borstal, detention centres and prisons were so much alike that they could easily be constituted into a single sentence. The detention centre regime with its emphasis on the 'short, sharp shock' was unique and, in theory at least, very different from Borstal and prison regimes which were geared more to training than punishment. To emphasize this difference, and in support of his belief that detention centres had become too soft, Home Secretary Whitelaw ordered an experiment with more military-style regimes at Send and New Hall, eventually extending the experiment to many other detention centres in March 1981. The penal lobby was hostile to this move, arguing that there was no evidence to support the idea that tougher custodial regimes would cut down on recidivism. As for Borstal and prison sentences, the Government did accept that there was some overlap here and it therefore suggested that they should be run together as a single sentence to be known as youth custody. Powers to introduce the new sentence are included in the Criminal Justice Bill now before Parliament (1982). The Government's continuing emphasis on youth custody has many critics. Why is so much effort wasted on arguing the virtues of one regime over another? Has the Government not yet learned about the futility of incarceration? These are the questions which worry the lobby.

The controversy over young adult offenders was paralleled by an even fiercer row over the operation of the Children and Young Persons Act 1969. Public anxiety reached such a pitch that the question was even taken up by a House of Commons committee of inquiry. As Opposition spokesman on home affairs in the mid-1970s William Whitelaw was particularly severe on 'hard young thugs' who were 'thumbing their noses' at the law. Not to be outdone, Rhodes Boyson MP declared that the 1969 Act was disastrous, placing children in the hands of ill-disciplined social workers who sometimes went so far as to attack policemen. It will be recalled that when a juvenile court issued a care order under this Act, it was local authority social workers – not the magistrates – who decided what happened to the child, whether to send him to a Community Home, to foster parents or even back home. What was being argued was that these social workers were abusing their power, were generally too 'soft', preferring nearly always to send the children home rather than into custody. Much was made of several admittedly tragic cases where children returned to their homes were subsequently ill-treated and, in one or two cases, even battered to death. Agonising as these cases were, they hardly constituted sufficient evidence to show that social workers as a whole were failing in their duty. True, it was generally agreed that social service departments did not adjust to their new responsibilities as easily as had been expected. No sooner had the 1969 Act arrived on the statute book than social service departments were faced with the reorganisation which followed the Seebohm Report (1968). Three years later came local government reorganisation. These changes imposed a considerable strain and if magistrates sometimes felt in the first half of the 1970s that social workers turned up in court with inadequate social inquiry reports, or had failed adequately to supervise those juveniles in their charge, their suspicions may well have been justified and criticisms along these lines were reasonable.

To admit this, however, was not to attack the principles of the 1969 Act or to demonstrate that its operation by social workers had led to a 'soft' attitude towards juvenile offenders. Indeed, supporters of the Act were keen to show that at the 'heavy end' of juvenile justice things had become tougher. For example, it was pointed out that the number of juveniles committed to Borstal rose from 818 in 1969 to 1,935 in 1977, and the number sent to detention centres increased from 2,228 in 1969 to 5,757 in 1977. This was a much faster increase than the rise in juvenile crime during the same period. Further, it was argued that if social workers had gone as 'soft' as their critics believed, how was it that the number of supervision orders (they replaced probation orders under the 1969 Act) made in 1977 was 18,152 compared with 21,652 probation orders in 1969? Surely the number of these orders which provided for supervision in the community rather than incarceration should have increased?

Looking back on the controversy over the 1969 Act it is difficult to sustain the popular image of 'hip social workers' who saw themselves as agents of radical social change struggling against a conservative magistracy. To be sure, like most popular images, this one has some basis in fact, but what hard evidence there is tends to show that not only did a majority of social workers agree with the bench about what to do with their clients, they were often prepared to recommend a custodial sentence in the first instance, before any alternative sentence had reasonably been considered or tried. What hope custody held out for young offenders is open to doubt. Leaving aside Borstal and detention centres, whose high reconviction rates were constantly showing their inability to direct their charges away from crime, Community Homes (they had 'replaced' Approved Schools) offered nothing that was significantly new. The same buildings were used, and in most cases the same staff operated a scarcely changed regime. All that had changed was the name, and how could it have been otherwise without a massive injection of new resources?

The growing use of procedures reserved to deal with the really difficult or unruly young offenders in the 1970s is a further indication of just how harsh the juvenile system was becoming. Apart from using assessment centres as an 'unofficial' means of containing difficult cases, social workers could apply to a court for a 'certificate of unruliness' and, if granted, young offenders were then sent to prison or to remand centres. The number of certificates of unruliness issued in the first half of the 1970s caused public concern, and even the Government was forced to admit that their numbers had 'burgeoned'. The way out, at least as the Government initially saw it, was to provide for more secure accommodation in Community Homes, and financial provision to local authorities for this was made available in the Childrens Act 1975. In future then, more really difficult young offenders would be dealt with within Community Homes while less would be sent to prison service establishments. In addition to this provision, the Labour Government also tightened up in 1977 on the regulations governing the issue of certificates of unruliness, and there was a noticeable drop in their numbers. Again, all this suggests that social workers in the 1970s had hardly gone soft on juvenile offenders.

There was also the question of Intermediate Treatment which many people felt was central to the success of the 1969 Act. The idea was that young offenders would stand a better chance of being integrated back into the community by working on local projects while living at home rather than by being held in institutions away from family and friends. Yet, by the mid-1970s very little Intermediate Treatment was available anywhere. Couple this with the Government's refusal to raise the age of criminal responsibility to 14 and its failure to phase out Borstal and detention centre sentences for those under 17, and it becomes clear that the 1969 Act promised far more than was ever actually delivered.

What is particularly important about the whole debate surrounding the 1969 Act is that towards the end of the 1970s there was a subtle shift in emphasis away from welfare to justice. The essence of the argument was that the welfare ethos had gone too far. Magistrates and social workers were so keen to get on with securing the child's welfare that simple justice was sometimes forgotten about altogether – due process, the principles of natural justice, were swept aside in the rush to secure the child's 'best interests'. This had to be reversed and pressure groups like Justice for Children began to gain in prominence. Particular emphasis was placed on the need for formal criteria at each stage in juvenile proceedings, the right of all parties to legal representation and in particular, following the collapse of the treatment paradigm, an end to indeterminate sentences, a central feature of our system of juvenile justice. Children no less than other offenders should be sentenced according to the seriousness of their offence and the exact length of that sentence should be determined by the courts, not the executive. Curiously, then, whereas it had been progressive in the 1960s to emphasize welfare against justice, the exact opposite was now the case; and not before time, murmured a number of old-fashioned magistrates.

As the Conservative Party in opposition had been among the 1969 Act's sternest critics it came as no surprise that when returned to office in 1979 it soon began work on measures aimed at reforming the Act. These were to include proposals to tighten up supervision orders, and a new residential care order which magistrates could use in certain circumstances against persistent young offenders. Although not the sweeping power to lock young children away which some magistrates had hoped for, it was at least an advance on what many magistrates felt to be Labour's unwillingness to 'back up the forces of law and order'. This criticism of Labour in the 1970s was not, as we shall see, entirely justified. More money was made available to the police between 1974–79, for example. On the other hand, Labour Ministers were reluctant to take on the law-and-order issue for a long time, either arguing that it was not a proper subject on which to have party dogfights, or that 'the problem' was not as bad as the Conservative Party made it out to be. Also, of course, Labour was embarrassed by its renewed stress on the link between material deprivation and crime at a time when its letter of intent to the International Monetary Fund (1976) meant public expenditure cuts in just those services which were designed to relieve such deprivation, a contradiction which the Party found difficult to reconcile.

POLITICAL PRISONERS

The problems of the young offender continued to receive a lot of attention, but the real focus of concern during the 1970s was the deteriorating situation in British prisons. There were different aspects to this crisis. To start with there was a growing number of political prisoners. As we have already seen, political prisoners are not new in Britain; there were both Irish and Greek Cypriots in Wormwood Scrubs in the 1950s and, of course, Irish prisoners have been with us for longer than the British care to remember. However, it was the conviction of the Angry Brigade on conspiracy charges which began the build-up of political prisoners in the

1970s. In the tense atmosphere which surrounded the Conservative Government's Industrial Relations Bill – five London dockers were later to be imprisoned for denying its provisions – the police alleged that the Brigade was responsible for a number of explosions or attempted explosions, including one at the home of the then Employment Minister, Robert Carr. Although not all the charges were eventually proved, Jake Prescott was convicted of conspiracy and sentenced to 15 years imprisonment in December 1971. Four of his co-conspirators were also found guilty and given long prison sentences a year later. It was then, not until after the Angry Brigade had been sentenced, that the first big IRA trial of the 1970s took place in England. This was over the bombing of a public house in Woolwich and in November 1973 resulted in a number of very long sentences. Four of the convicted, including the sisters Dolours and Marion Price, went on hunger strike for 213 days. Forcible feeding lasted 166 days. Their main demand was for repatriation to prisons in Northern Ireland, and after pressure from the Bishop of Derry and Lord Brockway this was eventually granted in 1975. Two other Irish prisoners whose demands included repatriation were Michael Gaughan and Proinsias Stagg. Both were to die in English prisons, Gaughan at Parkhurst in 1974 and Stagg at Wakefield in 1976.

The tension which surrounds Irish prisoners in English gaols is well illustrated by the disturbance at Albany in September 1976. The trouble started when an Irish prisoner was put in the punishment block for not cleaning out his cell. Six other Irish prisoners felt this punishment was excessive and eventually barricaded the landing to their cells. After the prisoners' refusal to dismantle the barricades a fierce battle took place in which several of the Irish prisoners were badly beaten. The Home Office claimed that nineteen prison officers were also injured. When a public row over this incident eventually broke out the Home Office denied that the Irish prisoners had been 'assaulted', but by that time there was a widespread feeling that the prison authorities had gone 'over the top'. This feeling was later endorsed, in part at least, in a report on the disturbances compiled by Amnesty, the National Council for Civil Liberties (NCCL) and the Howard League. The prisoners' feelings of injustice were added to by the draconian nature of the penalties later awarded for their indiscipline by Albany's Board of Visitors – some prisoners lost up to 630 days remission while sentences of between 13 and 19 weeks of solitary confinement were also imposed.

Apart from Albany, there have been other serious incidents. A number of IRA prisoners were badly beaten up after the Birmingham bomb outrage in 1976 and more recently seven Irish prisoners at Wakefield were punished for disturbances in the prison work-shop. There is no doubt the prison authorities have found contain-ing IRA prisoners difficult. By 1977 there were ninety-three prison-ers connected with Irish republican organisations serving prison sentences in England and Wales for terrorist offences. Seventy-five of these were in the highest security category, 'A', and many of them have been segregated at one time or another. This has been explained as a way of guaranteeing their safety. IRA prisoners, it has been argued, are unpopular and are more likely to be attacked, hence the need for segregation. The IRA, on the other hand, tend to see this as simply another form of discrimination.

In 1974 Labour's Home Secretary Roy Jenkins decided that hunger strikers were no longer to be forcibly fed. In future they would be allowed to starve, even to death. This decision was to have fateful consequences in Northern Ireland. Before the present round of troubles began Ulster's prison population was fairly mod-est. However, between 1968 and 1973 it trebled, and by 1977 had risen to over 2,500. This spectacular increase put an obvious bur-den on the already insecure system, especially before the purpose-built Long Kesh with its H-blocks became available in the mid-1970s. The early situation was further complicated by the separate regime required for those prisoners who were granted political or special category status. This had been agreed to in 1972 by Con-servative Northern Ireland Secretary, William Whitelaw. His thinking, it has been argued, was entirely pragmatic. Special categ-ory status was simply a bargaining counter in ceasefire negotiations with the IRA, not a principled stand on the rights of political pris-oners. What it amounted to in practice was that convicted prisoners – Republican and Loyalist – who were sentenced to more than nine months and whose political motivation was accepted by com-pound leaders were housed in separate areas, away from the main-stream of the prison population and, of course, separated from each other – Republicans and Loyalists had their own compounds, their own paramilitary command structure and so forth. Apart from their physical separation into these prisoner-of-war style compounds, special category prisoners differed from the rest of the prison population in other important ways. They were not required to work or to wear prison uniforms. They could also receive more visits than ordinary prisoners, have food parcels sent in and spend their own money in the prison canteen.

It was this regime, as it applied to both Republicans and Loyalists, that was condemned by Lord Gardiner in a report published in January 1975 which recommended that special category status should be ended at the 'earliest opportunity'. With the temporary ceasefire on which the original commitment had been based long since over, the newly-elected Labour Government took its cue from Lord Gardiner and announced that after 1 March special category status would no longer apply to new prisoners. Those already granted special category status were to continue to enjoy it, and in 1978 that amounted to 622 prisoners. The numbers may be dwindling, but in 1982 the compounds were still with us. The Conservative Opposition fully endorsed this new policy, and William Whitelaw publicly admitted that his original decision to grant special category status had been wrong.

The first Republican to demand special category status on sentence after 1 March 1976, and to protest at being denied it by going 'on the blanket', was Ciaran Nugent. He was soon followed by many others. The protest eventually involved refusing to work, refusing to wear prison clothes – each prisoner had only one blanket – and even refusing to wash or slop out. Human excrement covered the walls of the cells which were periodically steam-cleaned. There were no tables, no chairs, in fact no furniture except for a mattress. 'One would hardly allow an animal to remain in such conditions, let alone a human being', was Archbishop O'Fiaich's response to the state of the protesting Republicans when he visited Long Kesh in July 1978. By this time the organised campaign for what amounts to the return of special category status was well under way. Protest marches and demonstrations were organised and later, in February 1980, women Republican prisoners began their own 'dirty protest' in Armagh gaol. Further, and as Loyalists are rightly keen to point out, between April 1976 and January 1980 eighteen prison officers in the north were murdered by Republican forces.

An appeal by four Ulster prisoners to the European Commission of Human Rights was to fail in 1980 inasmuch that the judgment ruled that they were not entitled to political status, but the Commission did encourage the British Government to show more flexibility, arguing that simply because the prisoners' conditions were self-inflicted the authorities were not absolved from the need to compromise on humanitarian grounds. It was just the sort of flexibility which this judgment called for that was responsible, or so it seemed, for calling off a hunger strike by seven Republican prisoners in December 1980. Such optimism, however, was short-lived. The IRA clearly felt that the British Government later reneged on what had been agreed upon in December, and early in the new year the hunger strike was renewed. This was to last until the support of the Catholic community gave out in October 1981, and was to claim ten prisoners' lives in all, including that of Bobby Sands, who had been elected to Westminster as MP for Fermanagh and South Tyrone during his hunger strike. This desperate campaign gave the IRA an enormous psychological boost. It also helped their finances, or so it is alleged, with money pouring in from abroad, particularly from North America. Significantly, too, it put an increasing strain on Parliament's bipartisan approach to Northern Ireland. Some backbench MPs wanted Prime Minister Margaret Thatcher to compromise with the hunger strikers' demands, while the drift to the left among Labour's rank and file led some sections of the Party to question yet again what Britain was doing in Ireland at all. Mrs Thatcher was uncompromising in public, though significantly once the hunger strike was called off the Government did give in to some of the prisoners' original demands, such as the right to wear their own clothes.

The activities of the IRA fuelled demands for the reintroduction of capital punishment. As early as 1972 a Conservative backbencher had tried to introduce a hanging clause in the Government's Criminal Justice Bill. This was easily defeated. Not so easy to deal with, though, was Mr Teddy Taylor's backbench initiative in 1975. An ardent supporter of the newly-elected Conservative Party Leader Mrs Thatcher, Taylor introduced a Bill to restore capital punishment for murders involving the use of firearms or explosives and for the murder of policemen and prison officers. There was no doubt in whose direction Mr Taylor's measure was aimed. Labour opposed the Bill on several grounds, not least being Roy Jenkins' belief that to reintroduce capital punishment at a time of terrorist violence would only increase the tension. Associated with this line of argument was the growing feeling that just about nothing would stop committed terrorists like the IRA, so why create more martyrs? Taylor's motion was eventually defeated by 320 votes to 178.

Not to be deterred by his Westminster colleagues, Mr Taylor sought to commit his Party to a referendum on hanging. In this he did not succeed, even though Mrs Thatcher declared herself to be personally very much in favour of the death penalty in selected cases. The compromise decision reached by the Conservative Party was a commitment in the 1979 general election campaign to allow for a free vote on hanging, yet again, if it was returned to power. This commitment was subsequently honoured in July 1979. There was speculation that the murder of Airey Neave MP, one of Mrs Thatcher's closest advisers, in the run-up to the general election might push the balance of parliamentary opinion in favour of restoration. In the event, this turned out to be a false alarm for the abolitionists and the motion to reintroduce the death penalty was comfortably defeated by 119 votes. Interestingly, though, among Conservatives new to the Commons, 55 voted for the death penalty and 16 against, a higher proportion in favour than for the Conservative Party as a whole, perhaps an inevitable result given the party's recent attempt to emphasize 'law and order'.

It would be wrong to believe that the 'moral backlash', the determination to 'get tough' on issues like capital punishment or whatever, was only confined to the Conservative Party. It was after all a Labour MP, Peter Doig, who in a Commons debate on law and order (session 1977/78) had asked if it was too much to expect that someone who threw acid in another person's face should get the same treatment, and would it not be a good idea to put convicted bombers in a building and throw in a bomb? An extreme position, perhaps, but when Labour did finally get round to debating law and order Doig's more general wish to toughen up the penal system was not without support, for all the Party's emphasis on 'welfare'. (See Part Two.)

PRISON RIOTS AND INDUSTRIAL ACTION

The struggle over the prison system on the mainland in the second half of the 1970s never quite reached the same life-and-death proportions as in Ulster. On the other hand, there were major and violent disturbances which seriously undermined the credibility of the system. The first of these occurred at Hull prison in the autumn of 1976. In one sense, the facts of the Hull riot are not in dispute. A prisoner, it was alleged, had been assaulted by a prison officer in the segregation unit. Requests to visit the prisoner were refused, and this touched off the four-day riot. Although the prison authorities exaggerated the cost of the damage at the time, the prison was pretty well unusable by the time the prisoners surrendered. It is what happened after this surrender that became a matter for dispute. PROP argued that some prisoners were ill-treated on surrender, that their food was polluted with urine and that their private property was damaged. In a word PROP argued that there were two riots, one by the prisoners, another by the prison officers. The Government's internal enquiry agreed that there had perhaps been some unnecessary zeal which led to the disappearance of or damage to prisoners' property, but the allegations of the assault were unjustified. This conclusion was greeted with some scepticism, and mainly as a result of PROP's insistence – it was later to hold its own impressive public inquiry into the Hull riot (May 1977) – a thorough police investigation was held. Their task was not easy; the many prisoners involved had been widely dispersed and collecting the evidence would take time. Eventually, though, early in 1979 eight prison officers were found guilty of conspiring to assault and beat prisoners in the aftermath of the riot. All were given suspended prison sentences.

The violence at Hull was not entirely unexpected. Several organisations had warned the Home Office about the tension there, and the Board of Visitors did take some action, but it was obviously insufficient in the circumstances. This helped to cast further doubt on the value and fairness of these lay Boards, particularly when adjudicating on disciplinary matters between staff and prisoners. As far as most prisoners are concerned these Boards are 'in the governor's pocket'. The adjudication process appears to them to be stacked against them. Their sense of injustice is heightened by the fact that although Boards can impose very stiff sentences – one prisoner involved in the Hull riot lost 720 days remission – the right to call witnesses is circumscribed and there is no right to legal representation. There is also no right of judicial appeal, except on procedural grounds. What the Boards decide, then, is more or less final – only by petitioning the Home Secretary can their decision be over-ruled.

The uneasy prison situation was again thrust before the public by another riot in October 1978. Like Hull, Gartree was part of the dispersal system housing category 'A' prisoners, and when at the time it seemed that three of the four wings of the prison were under the control of the protesting prisoners, the police were called in to surround the outer walls. What is of particular interest about the Gartree riot is its cause, the belief that a prisoner had been improperly drugged by the prison medical staff. Although this specific case was never proved, the whole question of drugs in prison and their use for disciplinary rather than medical purposes had been causing concern for several years. The Home Office position on this is unequivocal: drugs are only used for medical purposes, they are not part of the disciplinary armoury. Many groups in the penal lobby dispute this, arguing that the use of the 'liquid cosh' is growing. There seems little doubt that in some prisons less powerful tranquillizers like Valium are used freely, paralleling the growing use of

such drugs in society as a whole. However, what concerns organisations like the Medical Committee Against the Abuse of Prisoners by
Drugging is the use of far more powerful psychotropic drugs like
Largactil. Evidence on this is hard to come by, but contributions to
the restricted *Prison Medical Journal* seem to throw serious doubt
on the Home Office claim that drugs are never used for disciplinary
purposes.[1] The high dosage rate in women's prisons, particularly
Holloway, is striking. This faithfully reflects the view that women
offenders are ill and therefore in need of treatment and cure, that
Holloway is a 'secure hospital' rather than a prison, a particularly
blatant attempt at ideological obfuscation which RAP worked hard
to expose in the early 1970s.

The conviction of eight prison officers in 1978 for their part in
the Hull riot was quickly followed by an event which might well
turn out to be even more damaging to the credibility of the prison
service. PROP describes what took place at Wormwood Scrubs on
31 August 1979 as 'systematic brutality'. The facts as PROP explains them are these. Prisoners in the maximum security wing began a peaceful protest about the withdrawal of certain privileges
normally available to long-term prisoners in dispersal prisons. This
non-violent protest was then interrupted by the arrival of the so-
called MUFTI (Minimum Use of Force Tactical Intervention)
squad, a group of officers specially trained to deal with prison riots.
In the ensuing struggle, argued PROP, dozens of prisoners were injured as the helmeted MUFTI squad ran amok with long staves or
pickaxe handles. As a result of the riot over 120 prisoners were dis-
ciplined either before the Board of Visitors or by the governor.
When PROP first broke the news of the riot and claimed many injuries, the Home Office flatly denied that any prisoners had been
injured. Later it admitted that a few 'very minor injuries' had been
sustained and finally it was forced to accept that 51 prisoners were
injured, plus 11 prison officers. After pressure from the penal lobby
to investigate the incident the Home Office set up its by now fam-
iliar internal inquiry. What this eventually came up with was evidence of incompetence, brutality and intrigue. The MUFTI squads
had been badly deployed, there was *prima facie* evidence of criminal
assault on prisoners and, perhaps most disgraceful of all, the prison
authorities had, in effect, sanctioned a cover-up. It took the Home
Office twenty-five days to find out just how many prisoners had
been injured! Following the failure of the police to find sufficient
evidence to prosecute individual prison officers, the Home Office,
remarkably, took no disciplinary action over the incident, though

the Governor of Wormwood Scrubs, Mr Norman Honey, was kicked upstairs to a desk job in the Prison Department, an oblique piece of scapegoating which pleased no one, least of all PROP which continues to call for a full public inquiry. It is difficult not to believe that guilty prison officers have gone unpunished.

The Scrubs riot did little to ease the already tense prison situation. Numbers reached a record level in 1978, and again in November 1979 when the prison population passed the 43,000 mark for the first time. Previous measures to halt this rise were called into question. So, for example, there were demands to strengthen the Bail Act 1976 which granted a statutory presumption in favour of bail; there were still far too many people in prison awaiting trial, some of whom would subsequently be found innocent or given at worst non-custodial sentences. There emerged, too, a note of scepticism about the growth of community service orders; perhaps they were being used not as an alternative to prison but as an alternative to less onerous penalties, say the fine. There was also a demand for new measures and, in particular, shorter sentences. It was hoped that the ACPS Report, *Sentences of Imprisonment – A Review of Maximum Penalties* would endorse this demand, as it did, though its recommendations were not universally popular.

What the Council proposed in effect was a new sentence structure based on the distinction between 'ordinary' and 'exceptional' offenders. The 'ordinary' offender would be subject to penalties with much reduced maximum terms; 'exceptional' offenders, on the other hand, would receive a determinate sentence but of any length – it would be for the courts to decide just how long the sentence needed to be to 'safeguard' the public. This new penalty structure was attacked from two directions. There was opposition from hardliners who felt that it was a deliberate policy to scale down sentences. Faced with a new reduced maximum, judges would almost inevitably scale down their sentences – and it is difficult to believe that the Council did not anticipate, even hope, this would happen. Outraged at such a possibility the *Daily Mail* claimed that the report was little more than a 'Rapists' Charter', a document 'saturated with intellectual dishonesty'. *The Daily Telegraph* was not far behind, warning its readers to be wary of 'this astonishing document' with 'terrifying implications'. More liberal opinion, while welcoming the likelihood of shorter sentences, was anxious about the 'exceptional offender'. How was it to be decided who was an exceptional offender? On the basis of his past offences translated into a prediction about his future behaviour? Who could reliably make such a prediction? There was no evidence that it could be done, offenders might stay in prison for years on the basis of some totally spurious prediction.

While Labour's Home Secretary Merlyn Rees was reassuring everyone, however obliquely, that the Council's Report would come to nothing, industrial relations within the prison system itself were going from bad to worse. In 1975 13 POA branches had taken action on 19 different occasions. By 1978 over 60 POA branches were involved in over 100 separate actions. The frustration felt by the service was acute. Staff working conditions were deteriorating because of overcrowding in the prisons, frontline officers felt abused by the press for the way they dealt with violent men, the 'bottom of the barrel'. All this while the Prison Department looked on, either unwilling or unable to promise anything better for the future. This is how the prison staff saw their situation and the POA's threat to step up its already damaging industrial action in the autumn of 1979 forced the Government to announce a full scale inquiry into the state of the prison system – the May Inquiry which resulted in the May Report (Cmnd 7673).

The May Report contained a number of important and practical recommendations. To start with what it had to say on pay and conditions was fully accepted by the Government which hoped that this would put an end to the POA's industrial action. In fact, quite the opposite happened. Disappointed by the award, the POA escalated its industrial action in 1980, closing prison workshops, suspending prison visits and even refusing to admit new prisoners into overcrowded gaols. For a period the newly elected Conservative Government had to call in troops to run a prematurely opened prison at Frankland in Durham and a hastily converted army camp on Salisbury Plain. The POA was also far from happy with the Report's call for an inspectorate independent from the prison service and directly accountable to the Home Secretary. This sounded to many officers, always sensitive to outside criticism, as if they were not to be trusted. More acceptable were those recommendations which taken together would help to reinforce the Prison Department's separate identity within the Home Office. Ever since the abolition of the Prison Commission there had been a feeling that the Department had been merged too completely with the rest of the bureaucracy, unwilling or sometimes unable to give the service the leadership it required. The Mountbatten Report had touched on similar problems in 1966. Important as all these highly practical considerations were, what was also of great interest at an ideological level was the May Report's contention that the language of the Prison Rules was seriously misleading. It continued to give the impression that reform and rehabilitation were still realizable goals, in spite of accumulating evidence to the contrary. May therefore suggested that the rules should be rewritten, the new official goal of the prison system should be 'positive custody', that was the least that could be hoped for.

It was, perhaps, this less ambitious view of the prison system which led the Home Secretary, when introducing the May Report in the Commons, to emphasise the value of alternatives to prison, and to suggest than in those cases where prison seems unavoidable, sentence should be as short as possible. To achieve this the Home Secretary at first relied upon judicial discretion and, when this failed, considered a scheme whereby all those prisoners serving between six months and three years might be released under supervision after serving just one third of their sentence. This early release scheme was strongly opposed by some senior judges and the Government has now (1982) settled for an option which allows judges, where they think it appropriate, to pass a *partially* suspended sentence whereby offenders are imprisoned for part of their sentence, say a quarter, the rest being suspended provided they behave on release. This procedure had been provided for in the Criminal Justice Act 1977 but had never been activated because the lobby was anxious that it could go the same way as the fully suspended sentence and lead to more rather than less people in prison. The 'taste of prison' might not prevent offenders from breaking the law on their release, they could soon be back on the inside, perhaps for longer periods if their new offences were taken into account. To say the very least, the case for the partially suspended sentence is not a strong one. Home Secretary Whitelaw's lack of political courage, his capitulation not only to the judiciary but also to vociferous handcuff-waving delegates at the 1981 Tory Party Conference, caused dismay in the penal lobby and, in the senior ranks of the prison service, open resentment. This was expressed in a letter to *The Times* by the new Governor of Wormwood Scrubs, Mr John McCarthy, who wrote:[2]

As the manager of a large penal dustbin I wish to write about the latest proposal of the Home Secretary to reduce the prison population . . .

The Advisory Council on the Penal System (1978) was extremely doubtful of the efficacy of suspended sentences in reducing the prison population. On part suspended sentences Mr Brayshaw, the then (1977) Secretary to the Magistrates' Association, echoed similar doubts, as did Mr Brittan,

Minister of State in Parliament (1979) and the Home Office's Review of Parole (1981). I have great respect for Mr Whitelaw's integrity and honesty and so I cannot believe that he is satisfied with the present proposals.

From my personal point of view I did not join the Prison Service to manage overcrowded cattle pens, nor did I join to run a prison where the interests of the individuals have to be sacrificed continually to the interests of the institution, nor did I join to be a member of a service where staff that I admire are forced to run a society that debases.

I am aware of the difficulties that the Home Secretary faces in reducing the prison population, but I find it difficult to understand why, if he genuinely wishes to reduce the prison population, automatic release on licence for short-term prisoners is not introduced. However he, for whatever reason, has not done this.

As it is evident that the present uncivilized conditions in prison seem likely to continue and as I find this incompatible with any moral ethic, I wish to give notice that I, as the governor of the major prison in the United Kingdom, cannot for much longer tolerate, either as a professional or as an individual, the inhumanity of the system within which I work.

I am aware that any gesture I would make would in all probability be futile, but if I do not stand up I shall be like a political party putting persuance of power before humanity.

Such outspoken criticism helped to keep pressure on the Government, which early in 1982 announced that it was considering the possibility of introducing parole for prisoners serving less than eighteen months. NACRO welcomed this, but pointed out that it would only reduce the prison population by around 2,000. Even this modest proposal may come to nothing, since the Tory Party is already reworking its law-and-order campaign for the next general election. Support in Parliament for the restoration of capital punishment has again been canvassed and Tory backbenchers made a determined effort to reintroduce corporal punishment during the Committee stage of the Criminal Justice Bill in March 1982. Mrs Thatcher too, has let it be known that she is taking a 'special interest' in law and order, so weakening still further the Home Secretary's room for manoeuvre.

JUSTICE?

As we have seen, from the exposure of the treatment fallacy a number of things followed. At a practical level there was the search for alternatives. More than just this, however, if offenders were not to be sentenced on the basis of how long it would take to reform or rehabilitate them then another measure must be found. In short, fenders should be sentenced according to the seriousness of their offence and for a determined period. Also, if they were no longer taken to be somehow diseased, people apart, then they should be treated, both during their trial and during their incarceration, according to the principles of natural justice. It is the emergence of this way of thinking, this drift in penal policy which we have been tracing. The force and wide appeal of this return to justice has been well summarised by A. E. Bottoms:[3]

By far the most important and influential alternative to the rehabilitative ideal, particularly in the USA and Scandinavia but increasingly in Britain also, has been the so-called 'justice model'. 'If we cannot ensure rehabilitation, and if rehabilitation in any case often produced injustice, then let us at least have justice' has been the cry. Justice in this context has meant primarily the *elimination of arbitrary discretion* by the decision-makers; so the main practical effect of the justice model has been in attacks on disparities in sentencing and in parole decision making, and in pressure for flexible penalties for specific offences. In some radical prisoners' movements, this has become translated into the slogan of 'the right to punishment'; the right that is, to be let out as soon as you have served a just sentence, and to serve your time without interference from psychiatrists and social workers if you want to.

At this point, two important qualifications are very necessary. To start with, in suggesting that the rhetoric of penal reform has moved from reform through rehabilitation to justice it is not our intention to suggest that there has been a clean and decisive break between these phases, or indeed that each successive phase has replaced all previous ones. That would be quite wrong and so, as our discussions of the May Report illustrate so well, reform, rehabilitation and justice still to some extent coexist. However, it would be fair to say that the dominant progressive rhetoric to emerge over the last decade has been justice. Second, our earlier discussion of reform and rehabilitation came to the uneasy conclusion that these labels were not much help when it came to finding out what was actually happening in the penal system, that they were little more than ideological constructs which obscured rather than illuminated penal processes. Can the same now be said of justice? To some extent, yes, though it has yet to be fully absorbed as official Home Office ideology (far from it in fact). However, to the extent that it is increasingly being taken as a progressive demand then plainly it is helping to dull our senses to what is really going on. To put the same thing another way, there was much talk in the 1970s about justice and alternatives, yet the prison population rose to record heights. This was not simply because of a rising crime rate – sentences had increased in length while the proportion of male offenders sentenced to immediate imprisonment, which had been dropping steadily since the early 1950s, actually increased in the four years after 1974. Further, many alternatives to prison, like the Newham Alternative Project, for example, were far too small to have any significant impact on the overall level of the prison population, while others, like community service, were often used not as alternatives to custody but in place of less onerous sentences, say a modest fine. That this helped to put increasing pressure on the prison system has already been demonstrated, and it can hardly be claimed that British prisoners in the 1970s, got anywhere near PROP's 1972 'Prisoners' Charter of Rights'. In short, the struggle for justice has a long way to go, in spite of all the progressive rhetoric.

POSTSCRIPT ON PRISON DRUGS

In recent correspondence with Lord Avebury, the Parliamentary Under-Secretary of State at the Home Office, Lord Elton, was more than usually frank conceding that prisoners are drugged for control purposes; that is, when their behaviour poses a threat of serious harm to themselves or others. This simply confirms what some groups in the penal lobby have always known, and it raises serious ethical questions for those who staff the prison medical serivces (*The Guardian*, 24 Aug. 1982).

REFERENCES

1. See, for example, *The Guardian*, 23 Oct. 1978.
2. *The Times*, 19 Nov. 1981.
3. A. E. BOTTOMS and R. H. PRESTON (eds), *The Coming Penal Crisis* (Scottish Academic Press: Edinburgh, 1980) p. 10.

Part two
THE POLICY PROCESS

Chapter four
THE HOME OFFICE: ADVICE AND SECRECY

For several years it has been recognised that the penal system is in a state of crisis. The prison population has reached record levels and this has led to severe overcrowding in outdated prisons. Conditions, admit the Prison Department, are 'an affront to a civilised society'. Partly as a direct consequence of this, morale in the prison service has reached an all-time low. As if this general demoralisation was not worrying in itself, discipline among prison officers has declined. Eight prison officers were sentenced in 1979 for their part in the Hull warders' riot while Parliamentary support is growing for a public inquiry into the unlawful killing of Barry Prosser in Winson Green gaol in August 1980. The normally cautious Howard League has become so concerned that it recently called for an independent inquiry into violence in British prisons. This loss of confidence in the prison system not only to guarantee 'humane containment', but, more important, to turn offenders away from crime, has not been matched by a sufficiently rigorous use of alternatives to custody. There are a number of reasons for this inertia, not least being the belief that the rhetoric which accompanied the demand for alternatives to prison in the 1970s was far too optimistic. Coping with offenders in the community, it is argued, is no more successful in diverting them from crime than incarceration. Thus the prison population has continued to grow, reaching levels which now, according to prison governors, threaten 'a major catastrophe'.

ADVICE

Apportioning blame for the present crisis is a constant preoccupation of those pressure groups whose business is penal policy, and a favourite target for attack has been the Home Office civil servants Any modest student of British government, so the argument goes, knows that whereas politicians as Ministers come and go, civil servants are far more permanent and it is, therefore, they who are really in charge; it is their ideas and priorities that ultimately determine the shape of government policy. This applies just as much to penal policy, it is suggested, as it does to any other area of policy. While not wishing for one moment to let politicians off lightly, or to protect civil servants from their share of the blame, it has to be understood that civil servants are not appointed for their specialist expertise, and so they too, like Ministers, though obviously less so because they have been in their departments for longer and therefore know some of the arguments, still have to rely on outside advice. Once this dependence is appreciated, apportioning blame for the present crisis in the penal system may not be as straightforward as some pressure groups would like to make out. In other words, it may not be the fault of powerless politicians or mandarin civil servants but a direct consequence of the advice that the Home Office has received from outside agencies. This line of argument, on the surface at least, seems to be supported by recent criticisms of ACPS and the Government's intention in February 1980 not to re-appoint it.

As we have already seen, the Government's first postwar advisory body on the penal system was ACTO, the Advisory Council on the Treatment of Offenders. During the first ten years of its existence its proceedings were unpublished, but by all accounts it was regarded as a prestigious body whose evidence was taken seriously by the Home Office. Of its public reports after the mid-1950s several have already been referred to. In 1961, for example, the Council skilfully marshalled the arguments against corporal punishment to head off a demand by Conservative backbenchers for the reintroduction of the birch. In a later report it took evidence which contributed to the abolition of preventive detention and corrective training in the Criminal Justice Act 1967. On the question of aftercare the Council seems to have been particularly influential, especially its second report (1963) which paved the way for a radical reorganisation of voluntary and statutory aftercare under the auspices of a restructured probation service (see Ch. 2).

If ACTO is to be criticised, as it can be, on the basis that the advice it gave to successive governments was not always based on solid criminological and penological research, its defence would most likely be that for most of the time it was operating such research was not sufficiently available. This would not be an untenable defence, since the Government's interest in these matters and the funds it was prepared to make available to universities for criminological and penological research were very limited, at least in the decade or so after the Second World War. Indeed, the Criminal Justice Bill 1947 contained no provision for such research at all, it was only thanks to a late backbench amendment that the Home Office was in future to be authorised to spend money in this way. Not that it amounted to much; a modest £1,500 for the year 1951/52. Although this initial sum was shared out between certain universities to encourage them to build up departments specialising in criminology and penology, the Home Office quickly developed its particular priorities and in 1957 established its own Research Unit, though it continued to divert a proportion of its funds to finance university research. (By 1968 the Home Office was making grants of £120,000 to universities and other outside bodies while the Research Unit's staff had increased to 23.) The creation of the Research Unit was the work of the Home Secretary, R. A. Butler. He felt that too little was known about the causes of crime and the effectiveness of various forms of treatment; the Research Unit was going to help put this right.

In addition to the Home Office Research Unit, R. A. Butler also encouraged the setting-up of a new and prestigious Institute of Criminology at Cambridge in 1960. The Institute's first director was Leon Radzinowicz who had for many years advised the Home Office on criminological research and statistics. The problems which surrounded criminal statistics continued to preoccupy the Government. To know the 'true extent' of crime and more about the ebb and flow of criminal activity was thought to be a crucial baseline for any future research and in 1963 the Government established the Perks Committee to consider what changes might be needed in the recording and reporting of information about criminal proceedings and related matters.

This expansion of research in criminology and penology was warmly endorsed by the Labour Opposition. The Party understood that more information was needed, that tackling crime and punishment required more than just an appeal to moral principles. There was a feeling, though, that perhaps the Conservative Government had not yet gone far enough, and in 1964 a Labour Party Study Group recommended that the Home Office Research Unit should be expanded and that following the success of the Cambridge Institute of Criminology two further institutes should be established, one in London, another in Scotland.

There was, then, a broad political consensus about expanding research and the purpose of all this research was also agreed. In the foreseeable future the Home Office Research Unit, the universities and so on would be feeding into the policy-making process – which obviously included advisory bodies like ACTO – a steady flow of 'hard' material which would better enable the Home Office to devise strategies to combat crime and, crucially, create a penal system which 'really worked'. The Conservative Government's 1959 White Paper, *Penal Practice in a Changing Society* (Cmnd 645) which set the research bandwagon in progress was a very optimistic document. There is, for example, even reference to the Cambridge Institute considering with academic impartiality the general problem of the criminal in society, 'its causes and its solutions' (op. cit., para 22). However, if this sort of scientific detachment and payoff now seem naive, the White Paper did at least realise that the sort of progress the Government had in mind would take time. The same cannot be said of its successor, published in 1964, *The War Against Crime* (Cmnd 2296) which announced the setting-up of a Royal Commission with the following terms of reference:

In the light of modern knowledge of crime and its causes and of modern penal practice here and abroad, to re-examine the concepts and purposes which should underlie the punishment and treatment of offenders in England and Wales; to report how far they are realised by the penalties and methods of treatment available to the courts, and whether any changes in these, or in the arrangements and responsibility for selecting the sentences to be imposed on particular offenders, are desirable; to review the work of the services and institutions dealing with offenders, and the responsibility for their administration: and to make recommendations. (Para 55).

Given that government had only begun serious research on any scale into crime and the operation of the penal system over the last few years, the Royal Commission's terms of reference were surely premature and impracticable. That at least was the view taken by one wing of the penal lobby. True, since 1959 there had been some advances, but as the appendix to *The War Against Crime* itself revealed, much research was still only 'in progress'. It would, therefore, be some years before such a 'fundamental review' (op. cit., para 54) in the light of 'modern knowledge' about crime and the penal system could be carried out. There developed a feeling that Home Secretary Brooke was simply responding to political pressure. That is, an increase in crime had fuelled public anxiety. What better to allay that anxiety than a comprehensive inquiry or Royal Commission into 'the problems'? It would demonstrate the Government's concern, its determination to do something. This sort of political manoeuvring was all very well, it might even help the Government to win the impending general election, but such a comprehensive inquiry was not justified in research terms, the necessary information was simply not available. It was this, no doubt, that led Leon Radzinowicz, who was to become a member of the Royal Commission, to argue that if the inquiry was to go ahead as planned, then it should at least conduct its business in a modern way. It should not operate as Royal Commissions had traditionally operated, by interviewing the usual pressure groups, calling for Home Office papers and cross-examining 'expert' witnesses. Nor should it rely on an enthusiastic but amateur secretary. Instead, it should have a secretariat made up of people with experience and knowledge who would liaise with specialist working parties made up of criminologists who would advise the Commission in specific areas, and where necessary commission work from experts in this country and abroad. In short, if the research necessary for the Commission's success was not yet available then at least some attempt to fill the worst gaps should be made by sponsoring projects while the inquiry was in progress.

This advice was not followed and Leon Radzinowicz resigned, and as we have already seen (Ch. 2), the newly-elected Labour Government abandoned the Commission in 1966. However, it is important to stress that although the Royal Commission had collapsed in some disarray because of disagreements over the scope of its inquiry and its methods of working, its decisive failure in no way undermined the optimism of the 1959 White Paper. Great progress could still be expected, given adequate research, in understanding the causes of crime and how offenders might be more successfully treated. To make sure this research was reflected in future government policy, Labour announced the setting-up of the Advisory Council on the Penal System (ACPS) in 1966. Slightly smaller than ACTO, which had been abandoned in favour of the Royal Commission in 1964, the new Council was weighed down with expertise. More than one-third of its eighteen members had academic qualifications in criminology and several had published extensively in the field. Their inclusion was clearly intended to guarantee that proper attention would be paid to research into crime and punishment and that this would produce more rational policies.

It was the Council's failure to live up to this promise that led to so much criticism, particularly from the Oxford criminologist, Dr Roger Hood.[1] The suggestion is that the Council's recommendations were not well researched, that it made important proposals based on untested assumptions rather than from empirical evidence. Take, for example, community service. The Council justified this new sentence on several grounds. In the first place it would appeal to those with economy in mind. Part-time service to the community was obviously going to be cheaper than imprisonment. For others it could be seen as embodying an important moral principle, reparation by offenders to the community. For others still, it would have the advantage of bringing offenders into contact with those in the community most urgently in need of help and support. This consideration was crucial since it points towards the Council's rehabilitative ideal, its belief that by being involved with those who most urgently need help the offender might somehow change for the better, be more balanced and responsible in his outlook on society. This transformation would be greatly assisted if the offender worked under the 'wholesome influence' of those people who voluntarily give up their time to help the underprivileged. All this sounds very laudable, argued the Council's critics, but where was the evidence to demonstrate that most offenders would, in practice, respond in this way? Or did the Council think that the scheme would be suited to some offenders rather than others, and on what evidence did they base this? The Council, it seems, had no hard evidence at all, it simply *assumed* that the 'average run' of minor offenders would react as predicted, and this untested assumption was seen as sufficient to sustain the recommendations of a major new sentence.

Similar guesswork, it is argued, also underpinned the ACPS recommendations on criminal bankruptcy orders which were introduced in the Criminal Justice Act 1972. These orders can be made against offenders if by their offences they have caused loss or damage to identifiable people in excess of £15,000. This provision was introduced partly in response to public indignation over those cases, say, involving fraud, where offenders can hang on to their ill-gotten gains even if they are committed to prison. More important than soothing public indignation, though, was the Council's belief that the new orders would have a deterrent effect. Potential offenders would no longer think it worthwhile to risk imprisonment *and* the confiscation of their criminal gain. This may seem a reasonable assumption about the behaviour of potential offenders involved in this sort of crime, but equally plausible is the assumption that such offenders normally operate on the basis that they are unlikely to get caught, and therefore the introduction of bankruptcy orders as an extra punishment will not necessarily deter them at all. On the basis of what evidence did the Council come down in favour of one assumption rather than the other? As far as one can tell, no hard evidence was available and so it must be presumed that the Council proceeded on the basis of 'intelligent guesswork'. The danger of doing this, of *guessing* how offenders might react to a new sentence, is well illustrated by the example of the suspended sentence which was considered earlier in a slightly different context. The idea behind the suspended sentence was deterrence: the court, though not wishing to immediately imprison the offender, could by the imposition of a suspended sentence show how seriously it regarded his offence. This offender would then have this 'hanging over him'. He would know just how severely he was likely to be treated if he came before the court again, and this, it was assumed, would help to deter him from committing further offences. While the failure of the suspended sentence must be attributed to several factors, including the frequency with which it was used by the courts, it also seems that the Government overestimated its deterrent effects. Offenders on suspended sentence came back before the courts time and time again. In other words, this apparently reasonable but *unresearched* assumption turned out to be far from accurate.

All this seems to suggest that penal policy-making is a very hit-and-miss affair, based more on intelligent guesswork than hard empirical data. Critics like Hood are particularly severe on the ACPS's record. After all, it was this body with its prestigious academics committed to criminological and penological research which was supposed to fulfil the promise of the 1959 White Paper. Is its failure, then, the main reason for the present penal crisis? Has R. A. Butler's promise of great advances in our understanding of crime and punishment been recklessly pushed aside? The plain answer is, surely, no. Indeed, it is about time the optimism embodied in Butler's 1959 White Paper is more openly questioned, and criticism of the ACPS re-evaluated in this new context. Briefly, the White Paper, and indeed much of what was being said in the late 1950s, created the impression that given enough resources criminologists would, in the long term at least, be able to come up with explanations of criminal behaviour in its various forms which would enable penologists to devise measures which would either deter or rehabilitate the offender. In the end, as it were, we would be able to develop a penal system which 'really works'. In retrospect such a goal was far too optimistic, not to say utopian. Criminology is no closer to understanding various patterns of criminal behaviour now than it was in the 1950s and penologists are left very much as they always have been, trying to devise sentences which deter or rehabilitate offenders without knowing much about why they behaved as they did in the first place. In these circumstances devising new sentences is inevitably something of a hit-and-miss affair, and perhaps the most constructive thing policy-makers can do is to adopt Barbara Wootton's modest proposal that we at least try to monitor new sentences when they come on line. Not surprisingly, it is just this straightforward pragmatism from a member of ACPS which so disheartens academic criminologists like Dr Hood who call for the application of more research into the formulation of penal policy; to proceed on a 'trial and error' basis is hardly adequate. On the surface this does not seem unreasonable; surely informed pragmatism can do as much harm as good. The problem, however, is that too much is claimed for criminological research. Barbara Wootton's question remains, 'But where, one may ask, is that "body of criminological and penological knowledge" to which Hood so lightly refers, which would enable anybody to predict with confidence the reaction of different classes of offenders to new forms of treatment?'[2]

The pretensions of academic criminology are best explained as a legacy of the optimism which surrounded the institutional expansion of the social sciences in Britain during the late 1950s and early 1960s. The 1959 White Paper classically reflects this optimism, a belief in the potential of social engineering. At that time, of course, criminal behaviour was still understood in terms of individual pathology, and it was the human or social sciences of psychiatry and psychology in an institutional setting which were going to rehabilitate offenders. More recently, and as we have already noted, this model of delinquency has been rejected; patterns of criminal behaviour are now explained in wider social terms and this has encouraged the move towards community treatment. Not, it is stressed, that this new knowledge any more than what went before it is likely to produce the sort of detailed knowledge about patterns of criminal behaviour which will enable Home Office policy-makers to devise penal measures which 'really work'. However, to the extent that the rehabilitative ideal to which successive governments have paid at least lip service has now been exposed as a sham, that many of our penal institutions are little more than violent, expensive and overcrowded human warehouses, then the least Home Office policy-makers could do would be to consider a decisive shift in policy towards alternatives to incarceration if what modest research we have on alternative sentences shows them to be no worse (or better) than custody.

Such research is available. The Home Office Research Unit's Report *Research and Criminal Policy* (1980) observed 'that research suggests that, as in the instance of the mentally sick, offenders – with certain exceptions – would do no worse in the community'. However, and crucially, the Report goes on, 'In this instance the direct connection between research and policy that might have been expected appears not yet to have been achieved . . .' (p. 5). Why? The answer to this fundamental question lies, in the main, outside the 'mechanics' of policy-making and we shall, in at least two different contexts, return to it later. In the meantime, though, it is fair to say that the present crisis in the penal system has not, in fact, arisen because politicians and Home Office mandarins have been fed the wrong information, that the promise of criminology and penology has not been encouraged to flower. What they and other social sciences can tell us is perhaps more limited than some optimists like R. A. Butler hoped for. On the other hand, there is more than enough information to show the need for a decisive shift in existing penal policy. Some in the penal lobby would even go so far as to imply that it is the very embarrassment which this information causes the present Government which has contributed to the decision to scale down the Home Office Research Unit and merge it with the Crime Policy Planning Unit.[3]

SECRECY

Not unrelated to the immediate crises are other aspects of the Home Office policy-making process which are far from satisfactory, including the often confidential and closed relationship between the Home Office and some of its advisers. It is difficult to inject new thinking when the same people sit around year after year operating on the same assumptions. For a pressure group like RAP for example, to find a legitimate place in the penal lobby in the early 1970s was far from easy. The Howard League, sharing with the Home Office a commitment to the rehabilitative ideal, was locked into the bureaucracy: its director had belonged to the same dining club as senior Home Office civil servants, its former chairman was also chairman of ACPS. RAP, on the other hand, was positively excluded and its challenge to the prevailing rehabilitative orthodoxy had to be articulated from the outside. A second example of the closed relationship which operates in penal circles concerns Lord Harris of Greenwich. Harris was a journalist with *The Economist* and a political ally and friend of Roy Jenkins. He was given a life peerage by Harold Wilson and taken into the Home Office as Minister of State by Roy Jenkins who was then serving his second term as Home Secretary. After Jenkins left British politics to take up the presidency of the European Commission, Lord Harris continued to serve at the Home Office until early 1979. He then resigned to take charge of Westward Television and, it transpired, the chairmanship of the Parole Board. The dismay his appointment caused is easy to explain. In 1979 the prison population reached record levels, the May Inquiry was in progress and from all sides came the call for fresh initiatives, including the extension of parole to help reduce prison overcrowding. The competence of Home Office politicians had been called into question by, among others, the *Sunday Times*[4], which delivered a blistering attack on Home Secretary Merlyn Rees for his inertia, for constantly 'wringing his hands' in public as if nothing could be done. The political appointment of his junior minister to the Parole Board just at a time when fresh thinking was urgently needed hardly inspired public confidence. The closed circle of penal policy-making had been maintained, the participants had simply changed places.

Another, if slightly different, aspect of the same problem is the close working relationship between advisory bodies and the Home Office. Barbara Wootton has recalled that in the early days of her service on such bodies the Department supplied a civil servant to act as secretary and then left the Council or Committee to get on and produce its report fairly independently of the Home Office. This has apparently now changed, civil servants from the Departments concerned now sit in on discussions and contribute. Wootton even remembers sub-committee meetings where committee members were actually outnumbered by civil servants. This is often justified on the basis that it prevents advisory bodies from suggesting to the Home Office (or any other Department) 'politically' unacceptable policies. They need to be reminded, as it were, what the 'policy boundaries' really are, at least as the sponsoring Department sees them. This sounds sensible. On the other hand, it inevitably means proceeding on the basis of shared assumptions, which is hardly a recipe for innovation. Of course this is not always the case, but it is a tendency which needs to be watched.

Not surprisingly, a closed policy-making process can all too easily degenerate into secrecy, and finding out in any useful detail what the inner circle are talking about or how they reached their conclusions is far from easy. So, for example, it is almost impossible to make any realistic judgement about the limited impact of the Home Office Crime Policy Planning Unit which was set up in 1974 to think about the long-term development and co-ordination of criminal and penal policy. It did publish *A Review of Criminal Justice Policy* (1977) which looked back over the policies of the previous decade, but it was mainly seen as an internal unit and was never intended to engage the public in an open discussion about the choice of strategic priorities. If closed or secret policy-making at this level is worrying, an even greater cause for concern is the secrecy which surrounds the day-to-day operation of the penal system, and in particular, prisons.

In the first place, the Prison Rules allow for the censorship of prisoners' letters. In the past it was not too clear what this involved in any detail, prisoners simply discovered what was or was not permissible through trial and error. Even a comprehensive knowledge of the Prison Rules would not have made the position clear. What prisoners really needed to know about were the Standing Orders and Circular Instructions which 'flesh out' the Rules, which spell out in more detail what can, in this case, be included in letters. Until very recently the Home Office was unwilling to make either Standing Orders or Circular Instructions available to prisoners. This was wholly unjust, it was like being asked to play by the rules by a referee who refused to reveal exactly what the rules were. After pressure from a number of sources, including the European Commission of Human Rights, the Home Office has now agreed to work on making its Standing Orders more accessible, so the one relating to letters and communication with the press, Standing Order 5, has recently been published. This could bring obvious benefits, but there are good reasons for not getting too excited. First, Standing Order 5 has a 'catch all' phrase which could easily prevent prisoners from writing to groups like PROP or RAP. Second, the Standing Orders are being 'filleted' with POA approval which, if the present rate of progress is anything to go by, is a process which could take years and years. Finally, the Home Office still refuses to make public its Circular Instructions. Such secrecy can hardly be justified on grounds of security, say anxieties about prison escapes. More important from the Home Office's point of view is obscuring what goes on inside our prisons. That is what the secrecy is all about, and this is why the authorities have tries their hardest, for example, to make sure that complaints, even very serious complaints, are dealt with internally, far removed from public view. The case of Sydney Golder shows just how far the Home Office is prepared to go in this context.

Sydney Golder was accused of attacking a prison officer during disturbances at Parkhurst prison in 1969. He denied this, but it was none the less written into his prison record. Mr Golder, not surprisingly, later came to the conclusion that this recorded allegation may have been decisive in preventing him getting parole. He therefore petitioned the Home Secretary for permission to contact a lawyer with a view to taking libel action over the recorded allegation. This first step was necessary, it should be noted, because no prisoner can write to anyone, with certain administrative exceptions, on legal business except with the express consent of the Home Secretary. In the case of Golder the Home Secretary refused his consent, and access to a lawyer was denied. In an attempt to circumvent this ruling, Golder appealed under the relevant articles of the European Convention on Human Rights and the European Court subsequently upheld his appeal, arguing that he had the right to consult with a lawyer and, in effect, have access to a fair and public hearing in a court of law, if so advised. This seemed an important breakthrough. In future, after taking legal advice, it was anticipated that prisoners would be able to sidestep not only the Boards of Visitors, but even the almighty, the Home Secretary, in their search for a 'fair and public' hearing. This interpretation turned out to be far too optimistic. In the first place, the Home Office openly flouted the spirit of the European Court's judgment by ruling that such access to the courts would only be available after the prisoner's complaints had been fully ventilated through all the internal channels, a procedure which could take a year, in some cases even longer. Second, until these internal procedures have been exhausted the prisoner has no right to consult his lawyer, that is, until his position has been exposed to and tested by those authorities who will at some later stage be a party to any litigation. In a very recent judgment the European Commission of Human Rights has roundly condemned this Home Office practice, arguing that prisoners should be allowed to consult lawyers even if their complaints are under internal investigation. A concession along these lines was granted by the Home Office in December 1981. The European Commission also ruled at the same time against those Standing Orders which prohibit prisoners from sending out anything for publication by the media or anything which attempts to stimulate 'public agitation'; such blanket censorship is simply not consistent with the European Convention on Human Rights.

What is involved in the Golder case and others like it is not only the struggle for justice, important as that is, but also the struggle to get things out in the open, to make the day-to-day operation of the prison system more openly accountable through the courts and elsewhere. That this is important is nowhere better illustrated than in the secrecy which surrounded the setting-up and operation of control units.

In a recent case Michael Williams, who was one of the first three persons to be placed in a control unit, sued the Home Office, arguing that it had, in so detaining him, behaved unlawfully. During the hearings his solicitor won an important judgment forcing the Home Office to make available to the court certain internal papers which showed just how the control units came into being. What is immediately clear from these papers is that there were differences of opinion. On the one hand there were three Home Office civil servants who felt the units should have some treatment or therapeutic value, that they should not end up as crude punishment units where 'troublemakers' were simply dumped for 180 days. Against this, there were hardliners who felt that the regime should be deliberately 'spartan', designed to teach those who suffered it a tough lesson which they would not be anxious to repeat. Concern over the inadequacy of ventilation in the proposed units, for example, was played down by one hardliner on the basis that anything which was slightly below par would remind the prisoner of the normal 'delights' he had forfeited. The same civil servant advocated a regime characterised by 'sterility . . . seclusion and anonymity'. The manner in which this disagreement was settled is an object lesson in bureaucratic intrigue. However, the papers are valuable for more than just this, since what they also reveal is a Home Office cover-up. That is, when it became clear to senior civil servants that the units would be difficult to defend they immediately set about trying to hide their essential details from the press, Parliament and the interested public. The Home Secretary was persuaded to play down their opening because 'intense curiosity' from the media would hamper their early development. Governors were told that censorship must be rigid while certain Home Office instructions were issued in a form which conveniently meant that they did not have to be lodged in the House of Commons library.

This cover-up is a serious indictment of the way the Home Office conducts its business at the very highest level. It confirms in a startling way the anxiety that it is all too easy for a closed policy-making process to become a secret one, and for a secret one to degenerate into a state of affairs where public accountability is something to be positively avoided. Perhaps most startling in this case, though, is the realisation that the day-to-day operations of the prison system are so shielded from public scrutiny that Home Office civil servants can hope to get away with such subterfuge. It is important to remember that these units were built, staff to run them trained, and prisoners allocated to one of them, all before the news of what they really involved was leaked to the press by worried relatives. While prisons remain such a closed book, civil servants will continue to act as if they have no one to answer to.

The formation of the so-called MUFTI squads is another case in point. The plan for the Minimum Use of Force Tactical Intervention squads was apparently prompted by the Hull riot in 1976. In his published report on that riot the Chief Inspector of Prisons argued that officers should have more 'advanced' equipment and specialist training to deal with large scale outbreaks of indiscipline. Acting on this recommendation MUFTI squads made up of regular prison officers began training at four regional prisons. The Home Office sought the advice of the police on what sort of equipment would be best. The first anyone heard of these squads outside the prison service was after the disturbance at Wormwood Scrubs in August 1979. It was subsequently revealed that the squads had been used on three occasions prior to this, at Gartree, Lewes and Hull.

The case for establishing MUFTI squads was never fully argued through in public, nor was their operational control. As a consequence, and not surprisingly, their ill-disciplined and apparently brutal behaviour at Wormwood Scrubs has been strongly condemned. It is at least arguable that they would never have been sanctioned at all if Home Office civil servants had felt obliged to justify their role in public. But, as we now know, they felt under no such obligation and so, as with control units, they were able not only to devise but also to operate a highly contentious and damaging policy under the protection of prison secrecy. In these circumstances it is no wonder that the Home Office gets so angry when that secrecy is breached. The case of Mr Jonathan Pollitzer is very apposite here, since he was a voluntary prison visitor at Wormwood Scrubs at the time of the MUFTI squad's raid. He soon heard what had happened, and quite dumbfounded by what he took to be a Home Office cover-up he made what information he had available to the media. For doing this, for being unwilling to confine his evidence to the Prison Department's own internal inquiry, he was immediately sacked.

The Home Office has an equally strong grip on full-time prison staff. In the first place, members of the prison service, frontline officers, the medical staff, the chaplain and the governor, all are subject to the Official Secrets Act. In addition, and arguably more important since the Official Secrets Act is kept very much as a background threat, are conditions of service which expressly stop staff talking to the press. So, for example, the Home Office moved quickly to stop more public comment by other senior prison staff after Governor McCarthy's courageous and outspoken letter to *The Times* in November 1981. Nor are these the only restrictions; the Home Office also insists that staff, however humble, are not allowed to speak on certain public platforms, say, where PROP is also providing a speaker.

In a curious way, then, just as the Home Office prevents the prisoner, by censoring his letters, denying him ready access to the courts and so on, from revealing to the rest of society what is happening 'on the inside', so it also gags its own staff. They can no more reveal to those on the outside what new and secret powers have been devised than those they guard under lock and key. The circle of control is complete. As the May Report so rightly pointed out, this has produced a very inward-looking prison service, made worse by the fact that so many of the service live 'on site' in prison accommodation. It is therefore hardly surprising that they have 'unrealistic' attitudes about a whole range of social and economic issues, that they feel beleaguered, as if they are 'standing alone' against the rest of us. Public criticism can provoke a very heavy reaction, particularly from the POA. There was, for example, the response to a BBC television series, 'Law and Order'. Outraged by the prison episode which depicted the 'liquid cosh' in use and a homosexual rape, the POA banned the BBC from all prison establishments for five months (who needs an Official Secrets Act!). Journalists, of course, are allowed in during normal times at the governor's discretion, but just what they can see, and who they can talk to, is strictly controlled.

Finally, even if the campaign against prison secrecy is understood as a way of making those who run the prison service more accountable for their sometimes fearsome policies as well as securing justice for the incarcerated, this is still only one half of the story. Such secrecy has an even more important ideological role. That is, it has helped to sustain successively the illusion of reform, rehabilitation and, now, positive custody. Had the prison system which includes Borstals and detention centres been less of a fortress system, then there is no way the rhetoric of reform, rehabilitation and positive custody would have endured. The lie would have been cruelly exposed. It is this knowledge which makes prison secrecy so valuable for those who run the system, enabling them at an ideological level to behave as if prisons are something more than warehouses even now, when the Home Office Research Unit has demonstrated quite the opposite, that to incarcerate offenders does little to improve them. To expose this official obfuscation, then, is what lies at the heart of the campaign against prison secrecy and, in theory at least, its success could help to achieve a fundamental shift in the direction of penal policy away from incarceration.

Ironically, the Home Office Research Unit has speculated on why its research findings about the relative futility of incarceration have not been translated into a shift of resources towards community alternatives which are arguably less damaging. The answer it came up with was that there was not enough public support for such a shift. To ask why this should be so, members of the Research Unit might start by looking at their colleagues in the Prison Department since it is they as much as anyone who have sustained in the public mind, by various mechanisms, including secrecy, the idea that incarceration 'really works'. To change public attitudes on this question in the present law and order climate will take time, but then political education always does.

REFERENCES

1. R. HOOD (ed.), *Crime, Criminology and Public Policy* (Heinemann: London, 1974).
2. In N. WALKER (ed.), *Penal Policy-Making in England* (Institute of Criminology: Cambridge, 1977).
3. *The Guardian*, 18 July 1980.
4. *Sunday Times*, 5 Nov. 1978.

Chapter five

PARLIAMENT AND THE PARTIES

PARLIAMENT

Parliament's contribution to the formation of penal policy is limited. This is not only because most members are relatively unin-
terested in the subject, but also because Parliament's role in the
formation of policy generally is only slight. To many people this
comes as something of a surprise. Parliament is seen to spend much
of its time discussing government Bills and therefore members are
somehow assumed to be important in shaping their contents. This
assumption is quite wrong. Most of the Bills which Parliament con-
siders are drawn up by civil servants and Ministers in the great Departments of State, say the Home Office or the Treasury, often
after consultation with advisory bodies like ACPS and pressure
groups like the Howard League or the Confederation of British Industry (CBI). Once they have been approved by the full Cabinet or
one of its many (and secret) sub-committees, Bills are then processed through Parliament. In that process, and this is what many
people find particularly difficult to understand, members can
change them very little; most government Bills come out of Parliament very much as they went in, at least in their essentials. This
government or executive dominance over the legislative process is
guaranteed by strong Party discipline and extends equally
to non-government or private members' legislation. Such legislation occupies only a tiny fraction of Parliament's time. Members
ballot each session for the chance to pilot through their own Bill.
Their success, however, is entirely dependent on the Government.
If their Bill finds favour with the Government of the day then it
stands a reasonable chance of becoming law, if not, then the
Government will simply block it. Sidney Silverman's private member's Bill in 1965 to abolish capital punishment, for example, was

successful only because the Labour Government wanted it on the statute book. If this had not been the case, the Labour Party's managers in Parliament could have easily found ways of 'talking it out'.

Such a strong executive, the fact that most governments can more or less guarantee their legislative programme, is seen by most commentators on British government as a positive asset. If it were different, if government Bills and policies were constantly being overturned or heavily amended in Parliament, then governing would be a very haphazard business indeed. This interpretation of British government, it should be stressed, in no way seeks to undervalue the importance of Parliament. On the contrary, in the face of such a strong executive its role is seen as crucial. However, its importance is not so much as a legislative assembly with a major part to play in shaping or amending government legislation, which is perhaps the popular view, but more as a forum where government has to justify and explain its policies, not only to Members of Parliament, but through them to the public at large. If Parliament is doing this, calling Ministers to account for their policies, scrutinising the administration of those policies in the great Departments of State, educating the public about the value of alternative policies, then it is fulfilling its main function.

As far as penal policy is concerned this process of parliamentary scrutiny and public education takes place in a number of different ways. First, there is what members do collectively, and most obvious in this case are the full-scale debates which accompany major legislative proposals, such as the various Criminal Justice Bills to which we have already referred. Although these debates normally last several hours and Home Office Ministers are quizzed by Opposition spokesmen as well as their own sometimes hostile backbenchers, the exchanges rarely develop into anything which could reasonably be described as thorough scrutiny. But at least the differing positions are reported and the central issues at stake, however badly put, are made known to a wider audience through the press, radio and television. As we have already been at some pains to point out, these confrontations rarely lead to great changes in the legislation under discussion. On occasions, though, and usually in the quieter atmosphere of the committee stage, some small concessions are made. For example, the Criminal Justice Bill 1966 contained no provision for an independent Parole Board. After pressure in Parliament an amendment to add this provision was accepted. During the passage of the Criminal Justice Act 1972,

Alex Lyon proposed that drunkenness should no longer be classed as a criminal offence, and this too was accepted by the Government. Both of these amendments had some cross-bench support which helped.

Because major legislative proposals affecting penal policy are comparatively rare, such full-scale debates are few and far between. In this sense the Home Office Minister has a fairly easy time, though he can be called to account by way of a full-scale parliamentary debate if the Opposition chooses to debate penal policy or an allied subject on one of the few days in the parliamentary session when it, rather than the Government, can decide what is to be debated. This is rare, but it has happened. In November 1977, for example, the Conservative Party chose to debate law and order which it claimed was under threat from vandals and muggers. The Conservative Home Affairs spokesman clearly held the Labour Government partly responsible for this decline into 'general lawlessness' and attacked their failure to introduce tougher penal sanctions, particularly for young offenders. This was the parliamentary occasion when Mr Whitelaw reiterated his plan for a 'glasshouse' regime for 'young thugs' in detention centres. The debate was widely reported and helped to keep the pressure on a Labour Government whose response to the law-and-order panic was shown to be ambivalent to say the least. Four years later, in December 1981 in fact, and as a direct result of the growing crisis in the prison system caused by serious overcrowding, the Labour Opposition turned the tables on Home Secretary Whitelaw by initiating a debate which was sharply critical of his failure to introduce more radical measures to significantly reduce the overall level of the adult prison population.

The fact that full-scale debates on any given subject area are so few and far between, that as gladiatorial displays they permit only the most general scrutiny of government policy, has forced Parliament in recent years to establish a series of all-party backbench select investigating committees which shadow the work of the major Departments of State, including the Home Office. These committees, usually consisting of about twenty members, call for papers from the relevant Ministries, bring in interested pressure groups and on occasions even interrogate the Minister himself. When these committees were first established in the 1960s on an experimental basis they were treated with suspicion. Ministers and civil servants did not welcome being called to account in a situation where careful questioning backed by well-prepared evidence could expose their policies to more searching analysis. As a consequence of this suspicion the original 1960s committees were abandoned. However, in one form or another – during the 1970s, for example, as the Expenditure Committee – they have revived, and on more than one occasion they have turned their attention to the penal system.

In July 1975, for example, the Expenditure Committee reported on the operation of the Children and Young Persons Act 1969. This Act aroused considerable public controversy and the Committee responded to this by carrying out a wide-ranging inquiry, taking evidence not only from the Home Office and the usual pressure groups, but also looking at community projects for young offenders both here and in Europe. The Report called for a number of changes in the operation of the 1969 Act. These included a recommendation that in certain circumstances magistrates should be able to impose acustodial sentence on young offenders, a power of course, which had been denied them under the 1969 Act. The provision of more secure units for 'unruly' children was also recommended. The significance of this Report, however, lies not so much in its detailed recommendations but in the attention it attracted. Most of the relevant social work journals carried something about its proposals and the Government, albeit reluctantly, agreed to debate it in Parliament. During this process, and under considerable pressure from the Conservative Opposition, the Labour Government was forced to defend its policy on young offenders. It later did this again in what was the formal response to the Expenditure Committee's Report, a White Paper taking up and answering the Report's recommendations one by one. The fact that the Government did not accept much of the Opposition's criticism, in that it was not immediately persuaded to implement the Report's many recommendations, in no way undermines the value of the Committee's work. A matter of public concern, much of it stoked up by the Conservative Party for electoral purposes, had been publicly debated and the Government of the day called to account. Parliament had performed its useful, if limited, function reasonably well.

The Expenditure Committee turned its attention to the penal system again in 1977. Then, as now, there was public concern over the growing number of offenders sent to prison. Overcrowding in local prisons was particularly bad. In an attempt to find out and publicise just how difficult things were and, in particular, to explain what might be done, the Expenditure Committee set to work and produced its Report in 1978 on *The Reduction of Pressure on the*

Prison System. Like its predecessor, this Report attracted a lot of public attention, both in the press and in the usual interested journals, and the Government duly published a White Paper in a detailed response to the Committee's fifty-two recommendations. It should be noted that the Government took its time over this – the White Paper did not appear until two years after the original Report had been published. This delay, plus the reluctance of the Government to find parliamentary time to debate the Committee's recommendations, prompted NACRO – it had submitted evidence to the Expenditure Committee – to hold a one-day conference on the Report to further publicize its findings. At the time of the last general election (1979), the Committee was inquiring into the position of women in the penal system. This was its last inquiry. The Expenditure Committee was disbanded in 1980 and replaced by a whole new range of investigatory committees, one of which, the Home Affairs Select Committee, soon busied itself with an investigation into the problems of the prison service.

The various committees we have referred to so far are official bodies, funded by public money and staffed by clerks to the House of Commons. It is this official status which explains their wide-ranging powers, to cross-examine Ministers and civil servants, to demand internal departmental papers and so on. In addition to these official committees, each of the major political parties in Parliament have their own backbench subject committees. These have no official status, are sometimes loosely organised, and their main function seems to be to provide a forum where members can meet other Party colleagues who share similar policy interests. Occasionally, of course, these committees can exert pressure on Ministers, particularly when their own Party is in power. Penal policy, even before the arrival of the 'moral consensus' and the parties' shared commitment to rehabilitation, had long been seen in Parliament as something which was best treated in a non-partisan way, and this tradition in the form of an all-party backbench Penal Affairs Committee has continued, even surviving the sometimes bitter debates over 'law and order' in the 1970s.

The Penal Affairs Committee rarely attracted large numbers in the past, except perhaps when capital punishment was on the agenda. More often than not it would lie moribund for several sessions, only to be revitalised by some major legislative initiative. It was, for example, active during the passage of the Criminal Justice Bills in 1948 and 1961. More recently, in 1975, the Committee again showed signs of life and established firm ties with NACRO which was then emerging as one of the more influential and energetic penal pressure groups. This close relationship has continued with the present Committee under the chairmanship of Robert Kilroy-Silk. In important ways this Committee has broken new ground, particularly in terms of the way it operates. The normal pattern for back-bench committees, and previous Penal Affairs Committees were really no different, is to discuss a fairly flexible agenda and then perhaps listen to some invited outside speaker. This helps to keep busy members in touch with informed opinion in their subject areas with the minimum of effort, but that is about all. The present Penal Affairs Committee has organised itself very differently, forming sub-groups which research into particular areas of penal policy and then produce and publish a report. The first of these, in June 1980, dealt with ways of reducing the prison population, the second with developing a strategy for young offenders. Although both reports received a good press, it is worth asking whether all the effort involved was really necessary. Has not the Committee simply duplicated the work of the Expenditure Committee which covered much the same areas? There is something to this charge, though it has to be said that the Committee's report on young offenders not only updated the Expenditure Committee's 1975 report, it also reached very different conclusions and in some ways was better researched. Perhaps the main criticism of the Committee is that occasionally its reports seem too close to NACRO's way of thinking, which is perhaps hardly surprising, given that its part-time secretary is also a full-time NACRO employee. In fairness to the Committee, though, other groups in the lobby like the National Association of Probation Officers and the Howard League are invited and do participate, so there is no deliberate policy to exclude other interests.

The question of parliamentary committees and their sources is an important one. A senior Home Office civil servant has observed that such committees – and he was referring to both official Commons Committees as well as Party groups – 'tend to feed on the usual sources of information, opinion and advice'.[1] From this it is possible to build up a picture of civil servants who have already consulted the ACPS, the Howard League and NACRO in the preparation of government policies, being bored by Commons Committees whose arguments turn on those self-same sources of advice. Even if this picture was essentially accurate it would hardly add up to a case for abandoning parliamentary Committees, however. The argument has always been that civil servants and Ministers are far too keen to keep their consultations with pressure groups and advisory bodies secret, shielded from parliamentary scrutiny. The fact that through parliamentary committees members can now have access to much the same information as their masters at least means that the policy outcome of such closed consultation can be the subject of informed and intelligent parliamentary discussion. Without such information, it is difficult to see how Parliament could fulfil its function of scrutiny and education in any meaningful sense.

Aside from all this collective effort, MPs obviously act individually in Parliament, and very occasionally with some success. Robert Kilroy-Silk, for example, was particularly worried in the mid-1970s about the number of children held in prison service establishments. He frequently questioned Home Office Ministers about the true extent of this 'scandal', and also managed to initiate a short debate in which he argued for a tightening-up of the regulations governing the issue of 'certificates of unruliness', which is how most children land in prison. The issue was then taken up by the Expenditure Committee in its 1975 Report and the regulations were eventually changed. Kilroy-Silk was actually asked to comment on a draft of the new regulations before they were published, and his suggested alternatives were accepted by the Home Office. Also active about this time was John Prescott. As the MP for Hull he was carrying out his own investigation into the causes of the Hull prison riot. He received some informal assistance from the Home Office and asked a number of parliamentary questions designed to help test his main thesis, namely, that the riot was caused by an increasingly repressive prison regime. Given the fortress-like style of the Prison Department his eventual report was credible enough, but he was seriously hampered by the fact that many of the prisoners involved in the riot had been 'ghosted' to outside his constituency while the POA, under the pretext of the Official Secrets Act, refused to speak to him at all. (He also had the tyres of his car slashed when on a visit to the prison.)

It perhaps goes without saying that the Official Secrets Act and the Prison Rules together throw a barrier of secrecy around the institutional core of the penal system which prevents members from carrying out another of Parliament's traditional functions, that is, the redress of grievances, the capacity to take up constituents' complaints against the bureaucracy. As we have already discussed in Chapter 4, for most prisoners just getting in touch with their local MP has its problems. To be able to correspond, for example, away from the watchful eye of the censor is one of the first difficulties.

Although there is much parliamentary talk at present about prison overcrowding, it is important not to exaggerate the amount of parliamentary time which has been devoted to penal policy in the past. One piece of research, for example, revealed that Ministers made only 35 oral replies to questions on penal affairs in the parliamentary session 1971/72 out of a total of over 4,500 oral replies by Ministers on all subjects. Debates on penal matters too, as we know, are few and far between. It is significant, for example, that the Home Office did not think that the Hull prison riot, arguably the worst prison disturbance since the early 1930s, was worth a parliamentary debate. True, backbencher John Prescott did eventually manage to squeeze a debate in towards the very end of the parliamentary session, but it lasted under an hour and started at 5.49 a.m.! Not surprisingly, only two members spoke!

However, having made the point that Parliament's interest in the penal system has been, comparatively speaking anyway, modest, and that its Members have been effectively barred from scrutinising its institutional core, it has to be said that the present crisis in the penal system is well understood by Parliament. The investigating committees have played a useful role here, sifting through a lot of outside evidence, bringing together critics of the present system and mapping out alternative strategies. Thus, if members of the Home Office Research Unit are wondering, as we suggested they were, why recent research indicating a possible change of direction in our penal policy has not been followed through, it is not simply because Parliament has refused to dig up the necessary evidence or failed to push new initiatives. Of course Parliament could and should do more, but it has at least sought to investigate and publicize the crisis which is about the effective limit of its authority.

THE PARTIES

The apparent and continuing wish among some Parliamentarians to remove penal policy from the arena of the Party dogfight, to have it considered in the quieter atmosphere of the all-party Penal Affairs Committee, cannot obscure the very real differences that have always existed on this issue, not only between the parties, but also within them, both in Parliament and in the country. The Conservative Party, and we have touched on this already, has been particularly vulnerable to internal quarrels over what should be the main objectives of the penal system.

Between 1945 and 1957 Conservative Party conferences did not focus directly on penal policy. This lack of attention is easy to explain. In the first place, the problems of economic reconstruction and foreign policy were far more pressing, and it was naturally these issues which dominated the agenda. Also, of course, the rise in recorded crime up to 1951 levelled off until the mid-1950s. It was the reversal of this trend, particularly the steady rise in recorded crime among the young, the so-called delinquent generation, which helped to push penal policy onto successive Conservative Conference agendas in the late 1950s and early 1960s.

The question is, what do these Conference debates tell us about rank and file Conservative attitudes towards the penal system at that time? Most obviously, perhaps, they show that ordinary Conservatives, then as now, take the penal system very much at its face value – it is primarily about punishment. This comes out very strongly in their early debates, as does the view that the available punishments are simply not tough enough. There are constant demands for the re-introduction of corporal punishment, the birch for young offenders, the 'cat' for adults. Allied to punishment is the idea of deterrence: the offender is punished so severely that he will not dare to repeat his offence, while those of us who witness this punishment will be deterred from breaking the law for fear of receiving the same treatment. The deterrent effect of capital punishment, in particular, was widely canvassed at Conference during these years, and in 1961 there was a very determined attempt to force the Conservative Government to widen the scope of its recently introduced Homicide Act 1957.

But what about the penal system and rehabilitation? Surely we are referring to the time of Home Secretary Butler's great leap forward, his plan, as outlined in *Penal Practice in a Changing Society*, to put penal policy on a more scientific footing, to make rehabilitation succeed where old-fashioned reform had failed? Had Conservative Conferences nothing to say about this bold initiative? They had, but in the main it was both sceptical and hostile. Rank and file Conservatives felt that the experts had already had their chance. When one speaker observed that 'sore backsides not psychiatrists, will cure big heads' (1961 Conf.) he was simply echoing in shorthand what many Party workers really felt, a profound distrust of the rehabilitative ideology. There was a widespread feeling among Conference delegates that penal policy should be determined more by something called common sense than science, by basic human responses rather than sophisticated intellectual arguments. Those 'intellectuals who lift up their arms in abhorrence at the thought of the return of corporal punishment' (1961 Conf.) were singled out for particular ridicule. It was just these people, in collusion with so-called 'experts' and 'professionals', who had made prisons like 'rest homes', even 'holiday camps' (1958 Conf.), who had continually stressed the needs of the criminal over the victim.

Although this emphasis on punishment and deterrence rather than rehabilitation has continued to dominate rank and file Conservative thinking about the penal system, the Conference debates in the late 1950s and early 1960s were sharpened by a sense of moral outrage at the thought of an increasing crime rate at a time of growing material prosperity. Delegates were mystified, and in an attempt to explain what was happening a whole number of 'causes' were explored from high divorce rates to the decline of the Church and the influence of the Bishop of Woolwich. But if the causes of the rising crime rate could not be agreed upon, there was at least some agreement among delegates about how to put it right. A first measure must be to strengthen the police force. Speaker after speaker argued that a better paid and equipped force would not only detect more crime, it would also deter more would-be criminals. But in addition to this, as we have already pointed out, tougher penalties were needed, this was no time to be 'going soft'. Unfortunately for Mr Butler, this is just what most rank and file Conservatives felt his rehabilitative ideal amounted to.

Not surprisingly, then, throughout the decade or so of the 'moral consensus' which R. A. Butler helped to inaugurate there is an air of betrayal at Tory Conferences. Delegates felt that their views on penal policy were being ignored, that their leaders preferred to listen to outsiders, to trendy progressives from the Howard League rather than to their own kind. In theory it was easy for the parliamentary leadership to ignore this criticism. Policy-making in the Conservative Party has always been the prerogative of the leadership, whether penal policy or whatever. The rank and file can make their views known on the issues of the day at Conference each year but these are in no way seen as binding on the leadership. In practice, of course, the leadership is often forced into making tactical concessions. So, for example, although the 'moral consensus' went unchecked, Conference pressure to do something for the victims of crime resulted in the Criminal Injuries Compensation Scheme which was introduced in 1964 (see Ch. 2).

Reading Conservative Party Conference debates of the late 1950s and early 1960s is a fairly straightforward affair. The offenders whom Tories either wanted to flog and punish or, if you happened to be a progressive, psychoanalyse and rehabilitate were, say, bank robbers or street assailants, offenders guilty of serious predatory or violent crimes which angered ordinary Labour Party members just as much as they upset the Tory faithful. It was this shared concern, a common belief that such crimes had to be tackled, that formed the basis of what agreement there was between the parties over penal policy. Even those people who believed that the problems of crime and punishment would never be 'solved' by 'objective experts', that parties would always hold opposing views about what should be done, nevertheless still believed that those who disagreed with them about how to tackle these problems were still fighting a common and easily identifiable enemy. This shared concern, however, visibly weakened towards the end of the 1960s and into the 1970s, when the focus of public concern began to widen to include not only predatory or violent crimes but also what were loosely labelled 'political crimes'.

This change is clearly apparent in the subjects discussed at Tory Party Conferences during this latter period. In 1968, for example, there is talk of a new phenomenon, the mass demonstration which shatters 'the peace of an English afternoon' and erupts into 'ugly, frightening' violence. The organisers are said to be professional agitators, some of them even foreign 'riff-raff' like the then student leader Tariq Ali, who should be deported as aliens. This mood of lawlessness and violence is characterised as one of 'the paramount problems of the age'. England is depicted as a state under siege where 'we have the argument of the jungle, where the argument is not that of the mind and intellect, but is that of the boot' (1969 Conf.). Conservative anger during the late 1960s is directed mainly at students, the long-haired, drug-taking perpetuators of the 'alternative society', the products of the events of 1968 and the anti-Vietnam War campaign. However, this preoccupation with youth – doped by welfare – and their apparent disregard for the rule of law is rapidly overtaken by a concern for what is seen to be a more worrying form of industrial lawlessness as trade unions take on Government, not merely by organising strikes but by openly flouting the law, in particular the provisions of the Industrial Relations Act 1971. London dockers are imprisoned, industrial action by miners and building workers convinces rank and file Conservatives that pickets are being allowed to 'terrorise and assault with impunity' (1973 Conf.). The crisis in legality, as the Conservatives saw it, was further compounded by the failure of elected politicians to obey the law when Labour Councillors at Clay Cross in Derbyshire refused to implement the Housing Finance Act 1972. In this tense climate it surprised no one when an old-fashioned pay dispute involving the miners and the Government was turned into a 'Who Governs Britain?' general election in February 1974.

From our point of view what is important about these developments is that those criminals traditionally attacked at Tory Conferences, the bank robber, the street assailant and so on, for whom the penal system was supposedly devised, are now joined by trade unionists and Labour politicians. So, for example, the 1973 Conference resolution on crime, after congratulating the Conservative Government on having achieved some reduction in the total incidence of crime, goes on to stress its concern at the 'unacceptable level of crimes of violence against the person and of vandalism as well as by threats to democracy inherent in attempted political and industrial coercion'. The resolution concludes with a call for 'even more effective measures to deter and direct all these threats to our Society'. For most rank and file Tories, of course, what the 'more effective' measures amounted to was an enlarged police force and harsher penal sanctions, a way forward which was soon to be vigorously endorsed by Mrs Thatcher who at long last told the Tory faithful what they wanted to hear. The wider political and economic significance of this changing Tory focus, and how it might be interpreted, will be considered in our next chapter.

To find out what the Labour Party thinks about penal policy is not easy, particularly as far as the rank and file are concerned. Between 1945 and 1980 Labour had only one Conference debate in which penal policy in any sense 'featured' and that was in the 1978 Conference on law and order. What evidence there is from the 1950s and early 1960s, and it is derived mainly from opinion polls, suggests that on capital punishment and possibly, though to a lesser extent, on corporal punishment too, rank and file Labour members were not too much out of step with their Conservative counterparts. This similarity was noted by the Director of the Cambridge Institute of Criminology who observed in 1964 that on these controversial questions there 'was a degree of affinity . . . between the alert Conservative ladies who, at the annual Conference of the Tory Party, made the life of Mr Butler so obviously uncomfortable, and the sturdy mass of trade union members . . .'.[2] To a limited extent this 'affinity' between the parties' rank and file may have stretched to cover a shared mistrust of rehabilitation too, though this was not the position of Labour's leaders in the 1960s, or for that matter of the progressive wing of the Party's rank and file. Their view of the penal system had a very different emphasis, and it owes much to Labour's only comprehensive postwar document on the penal system, *Crime, a challenge to us all* (1964).

This document is of particular interest for a number of reasons. In the first place, although many of its specific recommendations, on parole for example, were to become Labour Government policy in the 1960s, the Committee which drew up the statement was not an official Party committee. This, explained the pamphlet's introduction, was because this 'is not a subject on which there is great party conflict' and so, presumably, could be turned over to outside 'experts' who would 'assemble all the relevant facts, consider them objectively' and so on. This touching faith in the objective nature of criminology and penological research was in no way borne out by the document's frankly ideological recommendations which were, in important ways, in line with R. A. Butler's rehabilitative ideal, so helping to cement the emerging 'moral consensus'. There is, for example, clear support for the view that institutional 'treatment' can help prisoners to lead a good and useful life on release. The Committee was, it is true, at pains to point out that prisons, in spite of Home Office rhetoric, did nothing of the sort as things stood. Indeed, the gap between official theory and practice was probably greater here than in any area of Government activity (op. cit. p. 42). But this could be put right, prisons could become institutions of 'social learning' and their charges returned rehabilitated to the community. This emphasis on realising the 'proper role' of the penal system was stressed by the Committee (op. cit., Ch. 6) and the Labour Party was to pay lip-service to it during the 1960s, so laying itself open, of course, to criticism from rank and file Conservatives that Labour was the Party which cared more for offenders than victims, the same charge that had been levelled at their own Party in Government.

Labour's official response to the Conservative Party's emphasis on law and order in the early and mid-1970s was low key, and this helped the Tories to project themselves as the only Party that really cared about legality, particularly after the Labour Party bailed out the Clay Cross councillors. The difficulty facing Labour's leaders was fairly obvious. On the one hand, they were committed to the principles of parliamentary democracy and therefore obedience to the law had to be upheld. On the other hand, they were not in the business of either demanding tougher penalties against their own kind, for example trade unionists, or being stampeded into conflating 'political' crimes with what Eric Heffer called 'genuine crimes'. What Labour did not do, however, was to argue the implications of this distinction through, though it did appear to act on it. So, for example, it was these 'genuine crimes' which the National Executive statement on Law and the Community was concerned with, 'organised crime, theft and vandalism'. Labour believed, as it always had done, that such crimes had to be tackled, there was agreement with the Tories over this, whatever they might say, just as there always had been. What is more, Labour's official campaign notes for the 1979 general election set out to show how much tougher Labour had become in recent years in dealing with the crime problem, that it could no longer be described by the Tories as being 'soft on crime'. For example, the notes boasted that under Labour Governments in the 1970s the police force had been increased by 6,000 new recruits while the overall expenditure on law and order had gone up by over one-fifth in real terms. On the question of tougher sentences, particularly for the young, which seemed a preoccupation with the Tories, Labour had also acquitted itself well. The Tories' 'short, sharp shock' approach was sensationalist. What was really needed were more secure units to lock up the really disruptive offenders, and cash for this purpose had been provided by Labour governments. More detention centres for football hooligans were also in the pipeline.

When Labour's rank and file were at last given the chance to air their views on law and order at Conference in 1978 there was a fair amount of support for the Government's new tough image on the issue. Indeed, the tone of the debate at times suggested that perhaps Labour ought to be tougher still. In the case of some delegates this response showed all the signs of being something they had been wanting to say for a very long time, the 'moral consensus' notwithstanding. This confused and shocked the progressive wing of the Party's rank and file. Some found the Conference resolution which spoke about action to 'shatter' the sub-culture of violence in our society so foreign that they wondered if they had not come to the wrong conference by mistake, while others felt that the Party was in danger of succumbing 'to pressure from ratepayers' associations, Rhodes Boyson, the National Front and the National Association for Freedom'. Even more confusing, perhaps, was the distinction being implied between 'political crimes' and 'genuine crimes'. The Party seemed to be suggesting that socialists might reasonably turn a blind eye to law-breaking in capitalist societies where the criminal law is involved against working-class organisations, say trade unions, yet obedience to the law in other areas of activity, for fear of tough punishments apart from anything else, was essential. But was this distinction really valid? Had not Labour's welfare intervention on behalf of the young, for example, been inspired by a belief that capitalist societies create areas of waste and deprivation in our great cities, urban ghettos like Brixton and Toxteth which nurture crime? Did Labour's new-found commitment to law and order mean that these 'victims' of our unequal society were not to be punished more severely? Were the ghetto minorities, black and white, somehow less deserving than the organised trade union movement? Labour seemed either unable or unwilling to resolve this apparent contradiction and it struggled up to the 1979 general election talking tough, but never wholly able or, it is fair to say, wanting to reject its traditional commitment to crime prevention through welfare. In the end, Labour convinced no one, least of all the radical wing of its rank and file.

In what many people saw as a paradox, the 'get tough' attitude of both parties in the 1970s was accompanied by a growing disillusionment with the potential of prisons as a vehicle for reform or rehabilitation (see Ch. 3). This took some time to work itself through into the policy statements of the parties. So, for example, it was not until 1976 that Labour's Programme conceded that 'There is growing evidence that custodial sentences are not only expensive, but rarely successful as a method of reform...' (p. 92). The Conservative Party reached a similar conclusion at about much the same time when one of its study groups reported that 'The reform of prisoners, however, provokes concern, for we doubt if anyone who has examined our prisons, or for that matter the prisons of other countries, can escape the conclusion that prisons by their nature do not as a rule turn their members into law-abiding citizens.' (*The Proper Use of Prisons* (1977). Prisons, as far as the study group could see, were about punishment and deterrence and nothing else.

It should be obvious that this view of prison, symbolising as it does the collapse of the rehabilitative ideal as it was propagated in the 1960s, appealed to most rank and file Conservatives with their face-value interpretation of the penal system as being about punishment and deterrence. The argument that it was about something else called rehabilitation had never convinced them, any more than they had approved of Labour's welfare ideal which was not only 'soft' but in danger of overriding important principles of natural justice. These attitudes, it has been argued, and not without a certain amount of heavy irony, have placed the Conservative Party as a whole much more in tune with progressive penal thinking than at any time since the Second World War. Under reform in the 1950s and rehabilitation in the 1960s the Party's rank and file emphasis on punishment was seen as anti-progressive. Now, at least as a description of what the penal system actually hands out, it is acceptable, even laudable, in that it helps to break through the treatment smokescreen that surrounds the system, particularly our prisons. This emphasis fits in well with what those progressives who now favour the justice model are trying to do, that is, reveal the system as being about punishment pure and simple and on that basis argue for fixed or determinate sentences. Progressives and the Conservative Party are also in sympathy, so runs the argument, in their anxiety that the conflation of justice and welfare could undermine important legal safeguards, say in the handling of young offenders. There is perhaps something in this line of argument, but it is important to stress that those radicals who support the justice model would see the principles of justice extending into areas of the penal system where the Conservative Party believe they have no right to go, say internal prison disciplinary hearings. Also, of course, radicals have no desire to see welfare intervention withdrawn from those families whose children are in danger of drifting into delinquency. They do not see such intervention as being 'soft', as many Tories do, and who therefore use the demand for justice as an excuse to cut social services (For more on 'justice', see Ch. 7).

Finally, the formal conversion of both the Labour and Conservative parties to the idea that prisons cannot rehabilitate offenders and that therefore alternatives to custody should be encouraged is not normally regarded as problematic. Perhaps the only 'problem' seems to be explaining why the conversion took so long since the evidence, it can be argued, was there for everyone to see in one research study after another. This view is not uncommon but it has been challenged by some Marxists who believe that the demand for a shift away from custodial treatment owes nothing to research studies about reconviction rates or whatever – and this includes the work of the Home Office Research Unit. In their view, the inadequacies of institutional 'treatment' have long been known, but it is only now, at a particular historical moment, that there have been serious political demands for a move towards decarceration and this is a response to a fiscal crisis which is affecting Britain and other capitalist states.

Briefly, they argue that the size of the financial burden which has fallen on the British State, particularly since 1945, has grown rapidly, and for a number of different reasons. For example, technological progress has led to a large number of people being underemployed, unemployed or even unemployable. Unlike the reserve army of the unemployed described by Marx, many of these people are not pulled back into the labour market when production picks up, they are permanently detached from it and therefore dependent on welfare. This puts a large financial burden on the state. Welfare is costly but also labour intensive and, because of this, gains through increased productivity are scarce. In addition to this increased expenditure on welfare, the State has intervened to prop up and restructure industry (e.g., Leyland, Rolls-Royce), while at the same time paying out to improve the general economic infrastructure. Given the poor performance of British capitalism, all these expenditures can no longer be met, the state is facing a fiscal crisis which has forced successive British governments to slash public expenditure. It is this, say Marxists, which has led to the call for decarceration, and not some blinding liberal insight into the brutality and hopelessness of prison. Incarceration is simply too expensive. This is a suggestive materialist framework in which to set penal policy, particularly in the present economic climate, but it in no way explains why a policy which is an alleged financial imperative has not been put into practice. Indeed, prisons are fuller now than they ever have been and expenditure on them is more likely to increase than decrease. We must work towards trying to explain this in less obviously materialist ways.

REFERENCES

1. MORIARTY, M. J. in N. Walker (ed.), *Penal Policy-Making in England* (Institute of Criminology: Cambridge 1977) p. 139.
2. RADZINOWICZ, L. *An Address to the Howard League* (Sevens: Cambridge 1964) p. 9.

Chapter six

PRESSURE GROUPS AND PUBLIC OPINION

To many people the idea of public opinion may seem unproblematic. After all, it is argued, sophisticated sampling techniques now enable pollsters to measure public opinion fairly accurately on important subjects, say inflation or the efficacy of the penal system. True, pollsters can and do get it wrong now and then, but in the main they are not too wide of the mark, thus providing government with a reliable and important input into the decision-making process. Such a simple view of public opinion, its measurement and its influence, is highly misleading, and in more ways than one. In the first place, it ignores the fact that within what we loosely refer to as public opinion there are, on any one issue, a number of organised and distinct sectional opinions articulated by pressure groups whose influence on government is often far greater than the influence of that wider, more general public opinion which pollsters are so keen to measure and feed into the democratic process. Second, and arguably more important, to talk only about measuring public opinion is to ignore more crucial questions, questions which relate to how that opinion is formed and structured, how it is orchestrated and whose interests it serves.

PRESSURE GROUPS

Of the many organised pressure groups which seek to influence government thinking on penal policy perhaps the best known is the Howard League for Penal Reform. Established in the 1860s, the League takes its name from the great eighteenth-century prison reformer John Howard. Its early achievements were modest. Indeed, it might have faded away altogether had it not been for the outbreak of the First World War and the imprisonment of a number of middle-class conscientious objectors who willingly lent their voices to what was to become a growing chorus for reform. This eventually worked to the Howard League's advantage, thanks mainly to the efforts of Margery Fry who in the interwar years worked hard to establish the League as His Majesty's Official Opposition on all questions of penal policy. Never a large group, its current membership is around 1,500. The League is London-centred and financed partly by subscription and partly by donations from charitable trusts. Its members are predominantly middle class, and many of them come into direct contact with the penal system through their work as probation officers, lawyers and so forth. Although some attempt has been made to democratise the League's decision-making process, ordinary members do not have much say in determining policy. That remains the prerogative of the League's Council and Executive Committee, many of whose members are public figures with well-established contacts with those in Whitehall and at Westminster who run the machinery of government. These contacts have, at times turned into a virtual partnership, so much so that it has sometimes been difficult to determine for certain where the League's influence ends and where government begins. Take, for example, the First Offenders Act (see Ch. 1). The idea behind this Act was first floated in the 1950s by George Benson, a Member of Parliament and Chairman of the Howard League. To think through the implications of Benson's idea the Home Office arranged for ACTO to appoint a small sub-committee. George Benson and Margery Fry (she was still a prominent member of the League) were both appointed to the subcommittee, the outcome of which was the First Offenders Bill drawn up by the Home Office and piloted through the Commons by Benson, and through the Lords by Viscount Templewood, the Howard League's President!

To be sure, so close a policy partnership between the League and the Home Office was not altogether typical, even during the 1950s. There were plenty of times even then when the League's policy advice was politely listened to by the Home Office but then firmly rejected. However, it is important to stress that such policy disagreements in the 1950s were not about matters of basic principle. That is, the League and the Home Office, in spite of their many policy differences, shared the same ideological commitment to reform, held the same ideas about the potential and objectives of the penal system. When the ideological framework moved on in the 1960s, when it became progressive to believe in rehabilitation rather than old-fashioned reform, both the League and the Home

Office made the same transition; indeed, through their close personal contacts and their overlapping membership of influential advisory committees, they sustained and reinforced each other in the process. It is, then, in this ideological sense that the significance of the Howard League has to be seen in the 1950s and 1960s. It is not so much a question of asking whether or not it initiated or influenced this or that specific policy, though as we have seen it did wield power of that sort. Much more important is to understand how it helped to sustain at the very highest level the successive ideologies of reform and rehabilitation, hardly an enviable reputation in the light of what we now know was really happening in the penal system during those years.

It is arguable that the Howard League lost out in the first part of the 1970s. It was so plugged into the institutional side of the penal system, so determined to help devise policies to make prisons 'really work', that it failed to take on board the accumulating evidence that pointed towards the failure of incarceration, its inability to reform or rehabilitate offenders. This failure has been acknowledged, and to some extent the League has changed direction. It is now as much in favour of alternatives to prison as most other groups in the penal lobby, or that at least is its official position. Some doubts remain, though, not least among some of the League's rank and file.

The Howard League is sometimes accused of not 'doing enough' for offenders. What is usually meant by this is that the League spends too much of its time *talking* about policy to the Home Office, Parliament and the media, promoting ideas as it were, when what it should be doing is offering practical help to offenders. This criticism has some merit but the League could rightly argue that it has only a limited amount of resources at its disposal, that it cannot do everything, and in any case there are other groups in the lobby such as NACRO whose main function is to provide just that sort of help.

Established in 1966 when the probation service took over aftercare, NACRO (the National Association for the Care and Resettlement of Offenders) is a government-sponsored agency whose main function is to provide community facilities for offenders and to encourage other groups and agencies in the voluntary and State sector to do likewise. To this end, NACRO is directly responsible for a number of quite ambitious projects. For example, in conjunction with the Manpower Services Commission it runs a Youth Opportunities Programme in Manchester. Trainees are normally recommended to the programme by their supervising probation officer on the staff at the prison or Borstal where they are serving their sentence. They can stay on the programme for up to a year during which time they are given work experience and training and some further education. NACRO rightly regards this as one·of its more important projects at the present time when employment prospects for the young are so bleak, creating circumstances in which it is all too easy for young offenders to drift back into crime on release. Another factor which facilitates this drift is homelessness. Ex-offenders, particularly single ex-offenders, find it very difficult to get suitable accommodation. Too often they are forced back onto the streets with no base from which to search for employment and begin the difficult process of 'fitting back into society'. The Lance Project in Manchester and the north-west, set up by NACRO in 1973 and jointly funded by central and local authorities, has tried to eliminate this problem by establishing a varied network of hostels and bedsit accommodation to which ex-offenders are recommended through a central agency.

Establishing and manning a project like Lance ties up resources, particularly in terms of expertise, and NACRO is not always keen to stay directly involved with any particular enterprise for too long. Much better from its point of view is to hive off responsibility for running some of its many successful projects, as it did with the Hammersmith Teenage Project (see Ch. 3) which is now run by the London Borough of Hammersmith. This frees staff to set up or advise on similar demonstration projects elsewhere or to break new ground. One of the main problems with NACRO's demonstration projects is that in a number of fields, however successful they are and however much they encourage other groups and agencies to set up similar projects, the total and often temporary provision arrived at in no way matches up to the size of the actual problems. Take housing, for example. Projects like Lance, and the many other hostel projects throughout the country, provide valuable help and shelter for the homeless; but if the housing problems of the ex-offender are really to be tackled it will only be by making statutory housing provision more accessible. NACRO is increasingly aware of this and recently observed that 'the permanent housing needs of homeless ex-offenders . . . are likely to be met most appropriately by the normal housing system rather than by specialist accommodation exclusively for offenders'.[1]

At a time when prisons are so overcrowded NACRO's very practical help has never been more important. The difficulty is to ensure that its facilities, and those of the many voluntary agencies involved in similar work, are known about and processed in such a way as to make them readily available. This involves not only making them available to the probation service in both its supervisory and aftercare roles but also, crucially, making sure they are known to magistrates and judges who often impose short prison sentences because there is no alternative community 'package' on offer which convinces them that it will make a real difference to the offender's chances of getting himself together and 'going straight'. This is, of course, not an entirely new problem, but it is one on which NACRO has recently chosen to concentrate with the setting-up of several pilot 'multi-facility' schemes in association with local probation services.

NACRO is a large and complex organisation with, in one form or another, regional outposts. To run such an enterprise is expensive, and the Association's total income runs into hundreds of thousands of pounds. It received just under £400,000 from the Manpower Services Commission alone for the financial year 1978/ 79. It is difficult to see how such a large and dispersed organisation can ever be truly democratic, though it has to be said that attempts were made in the mid-1970s to involve staff more closely in the decision-making process. Staff teams within the organisation, say those concerned with housing or education, were invited to nominate a member to the central Policy Group which then issued policy statements for discussion and feedback. These statements, suitably revised or amended, were forwarded to NACRO's Council and, if agreed, became Association policy. The membership of the Council, it has to be said, is fairly predictable – interested Tory MPs like Mark Carlisle, members of the welfare intelligentsia like Professor Alan Little, representatives from the probation service and the Howard League and even an official observer from the Home Office. Given this sort of membership, and the simple fact that in the last resort it is a government-funded agency, NACRO's policies are never likely to be too extreme. This is not to say that it is a passive and uncritical servant of government. Such a view is far too crude. On many occasions NACRO has been highly critical of government policy, say over its attitude towards detention centres and sentencing. However, there are consensual limits and both sides know the boundaries.

The formation of NACRO's Policy Group, its publication in the mid-1970s of a ten-point plan for penal reform, its work with the Howard League in Parliament to bring about legislative change, all these activities show that NACRO is not just in business to offer offenders practical help. Equally important from its point of view is the job of influencing the policy framework within which that practical help is offered. To some extent this encroaches on what the Howard League has traditionally seen as its distinctive contribution to the penal lobby, that is, its role as the lobby's policy 'think-tank'. This encroachment is likely to continue and will probably develop into a very unequal partnership. It is difficult to see how it can be otherwise given NACRO's vastly superior resources. The Howard League's uncertain future is perhaps well illustrated by its very recent decision to focus far less on penal reform as such, and more on the criminal justice system as a whole. Penal Reform is therefore to be dropped from its official title.

To other groups in the lobby NACRO's considerable resources pose less of an obvious threat to their identity; indeed some of the smaller organisations gratefully plug into NACRO's services to supplement their own modest means. So, for example, NACRO's excellent information service is frequently used by Radical Alternatives to Prison (RAP) which would otherwise find it impossible to monitor the many formal changes which take place in the penal system.

RAP was founded in 1970 and grew out of the movement to establish a 'counter culture' which flourished in the late 1960s and early 1970s. Originally funded by Christian Action, it soon attracted support from young radical social workers, probation officers and lawyers. Today its constituents are not vastly different, although from a peak in 1972 of 600 its membership is now down to under half that figure. The organisation remains London-based as it always has been, though there are one or two regional groups. Since Christian Action ran into financial trouble in the late 1970s, RAP has been left to raise its own revenue and this it has done, though with increasing difficulty. If between membership contributions and the occasional charitable donation it can generate an income of around £8,000 then it can survive, but only just. Obviously, compared with NACRO, or even the Howard League which has an income three or four times as great, RAP's resources are meagre.

In the early 1970s RAP's contribution to the penal lobby at an ideological level was considerable. At that time, when the rehabilitative ideal was beginning to falter, RAP's unambiguous message, its conviction that prisons could not rehabilitate and therefore must be abolished and alternatives devised, helped to polarize opinion and force groups like the Howard League to re-think their commitment to prison and prison reform. This adjustment on the part of the League was never going to be easy, and in some ways it was made more difficult by the apparent totality of RAP's message, its determination that *all* prisons must go. So, for example, the League pointed out that even if alternatives to prison could be devised for most offenders, what about the 'really dangerous' minority? Surely prisons were needed for these offenders, or was RAP saying that they too could be safely coped with by community-based alternatives? Although RAP has *now* come to accept that there will always be some offenders who need to be imprisoned, it had very little to say on this important and practical question in the early 1970s, and what it did say was evasive. There were also other considerations which troubled the League. Prisons, or most of them anyway, might well be abolished in the long term, but they were certain to be with us for some years to come. In these circumstances surely attempts to make prison conditions more bearable were justified? RAP was not convinced, taking the view that all reforms which make prison life better are likely to shore up the system, to keep prisons in business for longer. This, as RAP later came to realise, was far too simple a position. What it needed to do was to distinguish between positive and negative reforms, that is, reforms that would support the prison system and those that would undermine it. An example of a positive reform would be a call for more psychiatrists. This should be opposed by RAP, because it would help to sustain the bogus rehabilitative ideal, the belief that 'treatment' is possible. A negative reform would be to lift mail censorship. This should be supported, since free communication with those on the inside would help to expose the brutality and repression which lies at the very heart of the modern prison system.

These differences over the progress towards abolition and, indeed, its very feasibility, helped to divide RAP from other groups in the penal lobby during the 1970s. There were, though, other and arguably more fundamental differences, and these stemmed from new perspectives on deviancy which were being canvassed by sociologists associated with the National Deviancy Conference. What these sociologists did was to criticise conventional criminology in two very basic ways. In the first place, they argued that most criminologists, such as those who ran the prestigious Cambridge Institute of Criminology, took the object of their study, the criminal, as given. They never sought to ask, as good academics should always ask, how the object of their study, the criminal, was defined or labelled. Second, they saw their task as openly correctional: criminals had broken the law, it was their business to try and find out why in an effort to put a stop to it; that, after all, was why government was so willing to hand over Home Office grants and encourage the growth of criminological research. What happened in the 1970s among certain radical sociologists was a determination to reverse these approaches. That is, they were unwilling to be used as crude agents of social control, to see their study of deviant or criminal behaviour as being geared to service the State's correctional policy. Second, and relatedly, they sought to look more closely at deviant behaviour, to explain why some acts and some people are labelled deviant or criminal while others are not. They did not find, as one is so often led to believe, that there is consensus about these things. Rather, they encountered a social reality in which diversity reigns, where there are many different groups, each with their own view about what should be defined as deviant or criminal. The problem is that this diversity, this *pluralism*, is not translated into a policy of tolerance. On the contrary, in any society there are usually some groups with more power than others to define what is deviant or criminal behaviour, and it is usually their views which get translated into the social and legal code at the expense of the weak and less powerful.

This view of the social and legal code, the idea that it does not reflect consensual values but rather the views and interests of powerful groups, helped to demystify the deviant and the criminal, to view them not as being ill and in need of treatment but as underdogs, the losers in a much wider social and political struggle to define what is acceptable behaviour. Further, as the 1970s progressed the idea that powerful *groups* were in control gave way in some quarters to the idea that they constituted a class *faction* whose members, although not themselves ruling, used the mechanisms of the state, including the criminal law, to sustain capitalist production in one form or another.

Much of RAP's literature came to reflect these new perspectives, though its radical message varied in emphasis, sophistication and intensity. This is not to say that all its members were committed radical pluralists or Marxists. Indeed, it is arguable that many of them were not, that they were driven on by 'humanitarian' rather than overtly political concerns. However, their willingness to go along with a critical approach towards the criminal law, to view the penal system in a much wider social context, inevitably led them into 'politics'. It was just this progression which most other groups in the penal lobby, notably NACRO and the Howard League, were keen to avoid, and it is this which helps to divide them from RAP and explains the mahy tensions which still exist between them. Thus, while RAP does not criticise NACRO's very practical emphasis or question the Howard League's humanitarian principles, to the extent that neither group is prepared to push the argument wider, to question the power structure of society then they are resolutely working in the interests of the powerful.

RAP's relationship with the Home Office is also strained. This is hardly surprising. Apart from the obvious fact that RAP is seen to be carrying a politically hostile message, its outspoken criticism of particular Home Office policies has not endeared it to senior civil servants; indeed, on occasions they have been advised not to attend RAP functions. So, to the extent that RAP has operated in the lobby, either as a campaigning group against control units or in a very practical way through its involvement with the Newham Alternative Project, it has always been on the fringe, constantly in danger of being defined out of the policy-making process. Unlike NACRO and the Howard League it is definitely not an 'approved' group. To remedy this RAP has recently placed some (mistaken?) hope in the leftward drift in the Labour Party and intends to plug into its National Executive Committee on Human Rights and Race Relations and also the Labour Campaign for Criminal Justice, which has already had some impact on Party policy by helping to structure Labour's second Conference debate on law and order in October 1981. Significantly, RAP's interest in the Labour Party is a far cry from the days of the 'counterculture' when involvement in the sterile machinery of 'bourgeois democracy' was eschewed in favour of working to transform the social order 'from within and from below', when 'grass-roots' alternative society projects left the conventional parties and Parliament to rot, or so it was thought.

The organisation for the Preservation of the Rights of Prisoners (PROP) was originally set up by ex-prisoners in 1972. Although not articulated in quite the same form or so consistently, PROP shares many of RAP's radical assumptions, arguing that 'we recognise the class structure of our society and see the penal system as designed to maintain that structure'. One of PROP's principal aims is to help 'develop this understanding amongst prisoners and amongst the working people of our country'. Just how successful PROP is at achieving this aim is another matter. The plain truth is that the Home Office does its very best to cut PROP off from its natural constituency, the prisoners. PROP's original demand in 1972, to act as a negotiating body for all prisoners, was rejected at the time and has not been seriously entertained since. Without this union function to fulfil, and the regular access it would involve, it is questionable how successful PROP is ever likely to be in 'educating' the constituency or, for that matter, in establishing just how much of PROP's policy is in line with what a majority of prisoners really want. This is not a criticism of PROP, or to deny that it has a lot of support on the inside, but just a straightforward observation of its organisational limits. There are other difficulties too, particularly over resources. To sustain its activities, PROP is essentially dependent on the financial support of its members, who include 'noncons'. It is nearly always short of cash and so more often than not what PROP really amounts to is an office and a telephone manned by a single, resourceful organiser who with the help of a few volunteers (they come and go) makes contact with prisoners and the press, puts together a regular journal and talks tirelessly up and down the country.

It is important to stress, however, that these difficulties have not stopped PROP from making a major contribution to the penal lobby. It is still the most reliable source of information about what is happening 'on the inside', particularly when there has been trouble. Whereas on such occasions the Home Office will clearly delay, confuse and even obstruct, PROP can usually be relied upon to piece together what really happened, as at Hull (1976) and Wormwood Scrubs (1979). PROP is, of course, well placed to publish its information. In the first place, it does not have to worry, as some groups constantly do, that such information as they do have might embarrass the Government and therefore jeopardize their 'good relationship' with the Home Office. Second, some members of the prison service are very litigious, thus frightening more 'prestigious' groups into silence; to put it bluntly, they have resources to lose. On both counts PROP has nothing to lose and it has on several occasions made very specific allegations about prison service misconduct. It has also made everyone in the lobby far more aware of the growing influence of the National Front in some of our prisons, particularly among ordinary grade prison officers. Given that some of our dispersal prisons have a black population of over 15 per cent (the figure for some Borstals is said to be over 25 per cent) this is an obvious cause for concern. PROP's work in this sensitive area is not helped by Tory MPs like John Wells (Maidstone), who issues racist disclaimers in Parliament but then goes on to talk about the plight, as he sees it, of 'small pink warders' being confronted by 'extremely làrge, tough, black' prisoners whose 'already fit' bodies are made 'a good deal fitter' by good food and physical jerks.[2]

One of the few 'prestigious' groups which has dared to step over the mark in recent years only to find itself the subject of a court action is the National Council for Civil Liberties (NCCL), or more accurately one of its legal officers, Harriet Harman, who found herself on trial for having shown internal Home Office documents to the press in the course of a trial over the use of Control Units. NCCL has a particularly uneasy relationship with the Home Office. It cannot be 'defined out' as being too radical; indeed, it represents just the sort of liberal democratic concern for justice which the Home Office is supposed to uphold. It is just this congruity which makes the Home Office so vulnerable to NCCL's line of attack, why it is so tetchy whenever the Council appears in some new lobby. NCCL's renewed interest in the penal system reflects the growing influence of the justice model, the lawyer rather than the psychiatrist now entering as expert. No doubt this new emphasis will bring some gains in the struggle to achieve justice for offenders, though it is important to learn from the American experience which has shown that legal victories, even if won in the highest courts in the land, are not that easy to translate into lasting gains in the labyrinth of the penal system.

The penal lobby has attracted the attention of many other pressure groups during the last ten years. Another product of the counter-culture, Release, has given valuable advice to countless people in their dealings with the police and the courts. Individuals, too, have played their part, like Peter Chapell who almost single-handedly mobilised the 'Free George Davis' campaign. More conventionally, perhaps, professional groups like the British Association of Social Workers and the longer-established National Association of Probation Officers have had their say on the important issues, like the operation of the Children and Young Persons Act 1969 and the Younger Report. Any detailed study would need to assess their potential influence. The Prison Reform Trust has also had some success in publicising the state of our prisons.

PUBLIC OPINION

All these pressure groups represent particular interests. They articulate particular points of view and very often what they have to say about crime and punishment is at variance with what we normally take to be public opinion, in its wider, more general sense, on these issues. This is especially true when it comes to handing out tougher punishments. The wider public takes the view that the penal system is more about punishment and deterrence than reform, and the tougher the punishment the more effective the deterrence. Groups like the Howard League and RAP who question this are dismissed as 'do-gooders', weak-kneed liberals who put the interests of the offender above those of the victim and the law-abiding. What are taken to be 'soft' punishments, particularly for violent crimes, are therefore far less popular than the 'tougher medicine'. So, for example, a Gallup poll in the 1960s found that out of those interviewed only 1 per cent were in favour of probation as a punishment for young men found guilty of robbery with violence whereas 14 per cent favoured birching and 21 per cent flogging. Obviously, public opinion about the desirability of one form of punishment over another for any given offence is likely to vary over time and, of course, the methods used to poll that opinion are, in truth, open to serious criticism. Even allowing for the necessary qualifications, there are few activists in the penal lobby who would seriously doubt what has been called the public's 'punitive obsession'. What needs to be understood is just how that obsession is sustained. Or to put the same thing another way, we need to ask ourselves the question, how is public opinion on crime and punishment so constructed and orchestrated? For an insight into this difficult question there is no better study than *Policing the Crisis*, which looks at the history of mugging.[3]

In August 1972 a man was stabbed to death in South London on his way home after a visit to the theatre. His death was later explained by the police as a 'mugging gone wrong' and was duly reported in the press as a new and frightening strain of crime 'imported' from the United States. In the following weeks and months a number of other muggings were reported and, in an attempt to stamp out what was seen as an epidemic of senseless violence sweeping Britain's cities, tough exemplary sentences were handed out to muggers. The most publicized of these were sentences of 10 and 20 years passed on three youths who mugged a man in Handsworth, Birmingham in March 1973.

The panic which came to surround mugging had obviously spread rapidly. As early as November 1972, for example, a public opinion poll showed that one person in six felt themselves likely to be at serious risk of being mugged. Not surprisingly, the same poll claimed that 70 per cent of those interviewed wanted the Government to act with a greater sense of urgency to combat mugging, and for 90 per cent of those interviewed this meant tougher penalties. It would seem reasonable to assume, then, that the harsh sentences in the Handsworth case were a direct consequence of growing public and judicial concern over the growth of a new and serious form of street crime which had first appeared in Britain six months earlier.

What at first interested the authors of *Policing the Crisis* was the speed and intensity of this reaction. They rightly point out that there is, in truth, nothing new about mugging. As a street crime most commonly spoken about as robbery with assault, it has been an unpleasant feature of city life as long as anyone can remember. So, why the great panic in August 1972 and thereafter? In an attempt to provide an answer to this mystery they asked a number of pertinent questions about, in the first place, the overall crime rate. Was there, they speculated, a sharp and disturbing rise in the overall crime rate which created a sense of alarm and encouraged a 'crackdown' by the courts? Answering a question like this is not as easy as it may seem. The official crime figures, which we have so far taken for granted, are highly problematic. For example, they say nothing about the 'dark figure' of unrecorded crime, nor for that matter can they even tell us the extent to which some crimes are more reported than others. Most obviously, perhaps, they sometimes accommodate changes in the legal definition of crime in a way which can be seriously misleading. However, allowing for all these difficulties, what evidence there is suggests that there was no alarming increase in the overall crime rate in the years immediately preceding 1972. True, the overall crime rate was on the increase, but it had been going in that direction for some time. What really matters is that it showed no sharp increase during the years in question and so the reaction of the judiciary and the public cannot be explained by reference to any objectively defined 'crime wave'. But what about those violent crimes involving robbery with violence which later came to be 'classified' as mugging, was there no increase here? Apparently not, a finding which leads to the conclusion that

whatever statistics are used, whatever the overall 'crimes of violence' figures, or more specifically those referring to 'robberies' or 'muggings', it is *not* possible to demonstrate that the situation was dramatically worse in 1972 than it was in the period 1955–65. In other words, it is impossible to 'explain' the severity of the reaction to mugging by using evidence based on the objective, quantifiable statistical facts.[4]

How, then, is this phenomenon, known to sociologists as a moral panic, to be explained – a situation in which societal reaction to a perceived series of events clearly far outweighs their actual threat? In *Policing the Crisis* the trigger point of the panic is taken to be the label itself, 'mugging'. What is argued, and convincingly, is that mugging already had a wider referential context long before August 1972. That is, the public had come to understand mugging not only as a street crime but as something which symbolised American urban decay. It conjured up scenes of racial conflict, dope addicts, police shoot-outs; a whole picture of urban violence which had been flashing across TV screens night after night since the mid-1960s. The idea, then, that mugging had now reached Britain touched off this whole referential context, it set the panic into motion, a process made easier by the close ties between the two countries, the belief that what happens in America will soon happen here.

If this wider referential context helped to trigger off the panic, it was also later used to sustain it. For example, the tough sentences handed out in the Handsworth case were justified in a *Birmingham Evening Mail* editorial on the grounds that we were edging too close to the American experience and something had to be done, the 'innocent' had to be protected on the streets. The media, of course, had a crucial role in the whole signification process, helping not only to import and contextualise the label but also to continually reinforce the panic, in the form of editorial comment, as above, and in the considerable space given to judicial comment. What judges had to say about mugging was important. Their tone, like their sentences, was almost universally severe. It is argued that the judiciary were in a 'get tough' mood. Judges seemed to share the public's anxiety that the permissive society had gone too far, that young thugs, black or white, had been let off the hook by the Children and Young Persons Act 1969. The time had now come to redress the balance. This resolve was reflected in many of the closing statements made by judges when dealing with muggers: society was seen as somehow being 'under threat'. Judges are commonly seen as the dispassionate upholders of the public interest, so judicial comment is respected, and the newspapers' willingness to reproduce it so regularly on the subject of mugging helped to reinforce and prolong the panic.

At this ideological level the police were not slow in coming forward. They, like the judiciary, had made public their view that tougher penalties were needed to combat violent crime and the mugging panic was taken as an indication of their several well-publicised warnings that things would get 'out of hand' if more convictions and tougher sentences were not forthcoming. However, what is particularly interesting about *Policing the Crisis* is its demonstration of how the mugging panic was, in important ways, not something that the police just reacted to but something they helped to create. The argument is that the police decided to target robbery with assault or mugging in south-east London in the early part of 1972 and special patrols were set up to tackle it, directed especially against black youth. The result was, not surprisingly, a number of mugging cases before the courts in the autumn of 1972. In other words, the police had been mobilised to deal with mugging long before the label was appropriated by the press and the moral panic under way.

What this investigation into mugging shows, among other things, is that the agencies of social control and signification, the police, the courts and the media, cannot be regarded as if they are

passive reactors to immediate, simple and clear-cut crime situations. These agencies must be understood as actively and continuously part of the whole process to which, also, they are 'reacting'. They are active in defining situations, in selecting targets, in initiating 'campaigns', in structuring these campaigns, in selectively signifying their actions to the public at large . . . They do not simply respond to 'moral panics'. They form part of the circle out of which 'moral panics' develop.[5]

The significance of all this is surely clear. Most members of the public have little or no direct contact with criminal activity, say, in this case, mugging. They have not themselves been mugged and therefore do not know how unpleasant an experience it is. Nor do they know for themselves how frequent muggings are or how widespread they might be in any given locality. To find out all this detail they rely, in the main, on the media. In the case of mugging the media created and sustained, with the help of the police and the judiciary, a widespread sense of fear which bore little relation to what was happening on the ground. The ensuing moral panic, the demand as measured in public opinion polls for more resolute government action, for tougher punishment, was, perhaps, a direct and almost inevitable consequence.

It is, of course, important not to over-simplify the creation of a moral panic, to presume that the media's message falls on an undifferentiated public with no preconceived ideas about crime and punishment. A moment's reflection will show this to be false. What the media has to say about any given crime or punishment will be mediated by individuals through a variety of social groups, say the family, colleagues at work or even the Howard League. Age too is important; the elderly are more concerned than the young about certain types of crime and in these areas are more likely to support calls for tougher action from social control agencies and the media. However, these considerations agreed, the realisation that we are dealing with a very complex process in no way undermines the central roles played by the courts, the police and the media in the formation of public opinion about crime and punishment, though these roles do not, of course, always come together to produce the sort of dramatic moral panic associated with mugging.

The construction of public opinion should be of more than passing interest to civil servants and politicians in the Home Office. It is, after all, they who are constantly arguing that reforms, say shorter sentences or more alternatives to prison, are impractical because public opinion would not tolerate more 'soft options'. If they could shake off their longstanding obsession with correctional criminology, the almost single-minded pursuit of one prediction study after another, and concentrate more of their research on wider sociological perspectives about, among other things, the construction of public opinion on crime and punishment rather than crudely 'reacting to it', then there might just be a better chance of moving penal policy forward. Perhaps this message is beginning to be heard. It was, after all, the head of the Home Office Research Unit who recently observed that the correctional emphasis of his department had deprived the Unit of collaboration with an 'important and critical' segment of academic opinion.

Not surprisingly, Marxists seek to locate any discussion of public opinion, and in particular the moral panic which surrounded mugging, into a wider and more complex framework. To take the argument as far as we have is, in their view, to go only half the distance. What they suggest in very simple terms is that the British ruling class, although a truly hegemonic class, that is, one which has imposed its own ends and its own vision on society as a whole, has been under pressure since the late 1960s. The hegemony it organised through the State, more by winning consent than by the exercise of coercion, has weakened in the face of Britain's stagnant, even declining economic performance. The easy consensus of the 1950s and 1960s is no longer possible. In these changed circumstances 'consent' has to be secured by coercion. Deepening social and political cleavages are being dealt with by noticeably tougher measures, whether in the form of more stringent laws against trade unionists or more intense policing of dissident minorities such as blacks, while at the same time, at an ideological level, such measures are being justified in the interests of 'law and order'. So, for example, the riots in Toxteth and Brixton, inner-city areas which are bearing the brunt of Britain's relative economic decline, were immediately met with a 'law and order' response, the suggestion that what we really want is a new Riot Act. This drift towards a 'law and order' society, the creation of an 'authoritarian consensus' has been taking place for well over a decade; and the moral panic which surrounded mugging – it was no 'accident' that the police campaign was directed mainly at blacks, or that it coincided with protests against the Industrial Relations Act 1971 – has to be located and understood in this more general context. Self-evidently, too, this context helps to give greater coherence to the changing focus of Tory Party Conference debates after 1968, the progress from a fairly narrow concern with predatory or violent crimes to a more general concern with what was taken to be a 'crisis in legality'. The right wing of the Labour Party, of course, shared this concern and played a willing part in the construction of the 'authoritarian consensus', actually going into the 1979 general election boasting about their tough stance on 'law and order'. Labour's left, though deeply suspicious of this stance and arguing passionately for welfare, had no clear analysis of why or how the consensus was being reconstructed or how it might be opposed.

Finally, Marxists would argue, and this is of direct concern to the penal lobby, that in order to maintain its credibility as a government truly concerned with 'law and order' the present Conservative administration cannot be seen to be going soft on prisoners by advocating decarceration, even though the savings involved would help the State in its present fiscal crisis. It may make gestures in that direction, but they will never amount to much. Having helped to create the 'authoritarian consensus' the Government cannot so easily ditch it; not, of course, that it wants to, since at an ideological level it is an indispensable instrument in policing the present crisis as spending cuts lowering the social wage begin to bite deeper, and social discontent in British cities continues to fester.

REFERENCES

1. NACRO, *Annual Report 1979/80* (London, 1980).
2. HANSARD, 18 Feb. 1977.
3. S. HALL *et al.*, *Policing the Crisis* (Macmillan: London, 1978).
4. ibid., p. 11.
5. ibid., p. 52.

Part three
ALTERNATIVES

Chapter seven

REPEATING THE OBVIOUS AND THE UNLIKELY

Before suggesting what needs to be done, it is important to recall the historical context of what we now understand as prisons. As institutions where offenders are sent to be punished and corrected, prisons are very much the product of the Industrial Revolution. Built in or close to large and expanding areas of urban population, prisons like Pentonville (1842), Leeds (1840) and Leicester (1850) were intended as ever-present reminders to those who broke the social contract that punishment now involved incarceration and correction behind their awesome towering walls. Of course there had been prisons before the Industrial Revolution, but they had been used mainly for those on remand and for debtors who were normally held under more flexible conditions. Relatively few offenders were sentenced to prison as such, they were more likely to be transported or to suffer bodily punishments, say whipping or branding or even hanging. During the course of the Industrial Revolution this emphasis began to change. There was a shift away from punishments directed at the body to punishments directed at the mind. This reflected a feeling, an optimism almost, that under the right conditions men's minds might be recast, that offenders could be resocialised to lead a good and useful life. This great enterprise was entrusted to new model prisons using highly developed systems or technologies of control based on surveillance, classification and instruction. Right from the start there had to be adjustments, 'reforms' to get things right.

Prison reform, then, is as old as the modern prison itself. It is also futile; no amount of reform will ever produce a prison system which 'really works', one that is capable of 'transforming' offenders, call it rehabilitation or whatever. The simple and sad truth is that our 'modern' prisons are what they always have been, little more than human warehouses. Offenders are simply stored there, and brutalised by the experience. They are not the only ones who suffer in this way, those who guard them are also brutalised while society, under the illusion that something constructive is being done 'on the inside', is persuaded to tolerate a wholesale disregard for human rights. Faced with this situation the main thrust of any alternative penal policy must be, in the short term anyway, to reduce the present prison population which in July 1981 reached the record figure of 45,500.

KEEPING OFFENDERS OUT OF PRISON

There are a number of obvious ways in which this might be done. In the first place, there are certain categories of offenders who should simply not be imprisoned at all. Take, for example, the mentally ill. In recent years local psychiatric hospitals have become increasingly reluctant to admit 'difficult' mentally ill offenders. As a consequence, and because they are not dangerous enough to be sent to a special secure psychiatric hospital, these would-be patients are dumped – there is no other word for it – in prison. Not surprisingly, the prison medical service has opposed this practice and successive governments have been forced to concede that it is no part of a civilised society to allow prisons to be used as 'receptacles' for those whom no other agency in society will accept. This may sound positive enough, but in practice very little has been done. Indeed, one plan (though not necessarily the best alternative for 'difficult' mentally ill offenders), the provision of regional secure units, was actually subverted by regional health authorities who spent the money allocated to them for the units in other ways; in some cases the money was not even spent on mental health! To treat mentally ill prisoners with such cynical disregard is quite unacceptable; the National Health Service should face up to its responsibilities in this area. It is possible to devise constructive alternatives to prison for these offenders and they should be made available as a matter of some urgency.

If prison is no place for the mentally ill, then it is certainly no place for the habitual drunken offender. Since 1977 being drunk and disorderly is not directly punishable by imprisonment. What happens now is that offenders are fined instead, but even when the sum involved is only a nominal amount it is rarely paid and habitual drunken offenders are usually picked up a few days or weeks later in much the same state as before, a pointless cycle which is broken only when they are eventually imprisoned for non-payment of fines. Prison can do little for these offenders and this was recognised in the Criminal Justice Act 1972 which empowered the Government to set up detoxification centres where offenders could 'dry out' as an alternative to imprisonment. Regrettably, progress has been slow on this front. Only two detoxification centres have been opened so far and so prison receptions for drunkenness-related offences have continued to be high. In 1978, for example, the figure was not far short of 3,000. The problem seems to be twofold. To start with, the 'success rate' of these centres has been called into question. This is understandable but in some ways unhelpful, since there is no 'magic cure' for habitually drunken offenders and the Government probably expected more from these centres than they could ever hope to deliver. Second, and relatedly, the centres have turned out to be expensive to run but, as groups like RAP have pointed out, they need not be: an acceptable caring environment can be achieved without elaborate medical resources. Voluntary groups securely funded by central or local government could well provide the sort of continuous support which is needed at a very reasonable cost.

If the prison regime is quite unsuited to the special needs of the mentally ill and the habitually drunken offender, it does little either for the petty persistent offender, the small-time corner-café 'criminal' who is nearly always broke. Such offenders are rarely sentenced to more than a few months and could easily be diverted from the prison system without any real danger to the public. More often than not, their contact with the law arises from the difficult business of making a living if you happen to be homeless or jobless, or lacking in the sort of social skills which most of us take for granted. For these offenders, attending Day Training Centres (set up under the Criminal Justice Act 1972) as a condition of probation, or a helping hand under supervision in one of NACRO's housing or employment schemes is what is wanted, not the sledgehammer of prison.

Imprisoning maintenance defaulters is another example of overkill. In 1978, 2,564 men were received into prison for failing to pay maintenance, many of them simply through lack of the necessary financial resources. The Payne Committee argued that to imprison such offenders 'is morally capricious, economically wasteful, socially harmful, administratively burdensome and juridically wrong'.[1] The problem often is that the defendant's ability to pay is never properly assessed. It is, in fact, only rarely that his eventual default is due to 'wilful refusal'. The suggestion that an Enforcement

Office should be set up, better able than the courts to look into the defaulter's affairs, is surely worth exploring. Provided it did not set out to control offenders' affairs too closely, and so become oppressive, it would obviously be preferable to imprisonment which costs the State large sums of money while at the same time contributing nothing towards the upkeep of the defaulter's family.

A similar strategy should be used for fine defaulters in general. It is a sad reflection on our criminal justice system when it is admitted that the level at which magistrates set fines is a mixture of bluff and chance. A much more thorough attempt must be made to decide what offenders can really afford or else fines will increasingly become not an alternative sentence to prison but the first step on the way towards it. To some extent, of course, it has already become just that for some petty persistent offenders as well as the habitually drunk; very often this is how they are 'staged' or processed through the system to eventually end up 'on the inside'. The same is also true for prostitutes. Although prostitution is not itself an offence, soliciting is, and for a third offence it can carry a fine of up to £200 and/or three months imprisonment. Even the male-dominated Home Offfice Working Party on Vagrancy and Street Offences, although by no means sympathetic to the 'problem' of prostitution, agreed that any rehabilitative value prison might have for prostitutes was limited since, 'It is usually the least successful prostitutes who get sent to prison – a prostitute who becomes successfully established is less likely to have to ply her trade in the streets – and their problems are so great that it is difficult to do anything to help them in a short period in prison.' (Para 251.) Given this opinion, the fact that even those who still cling fast to the rehabilitative ideal can see no point in imprisoning prostitutes for the short length of time their offence warrants, incarceration as a sentence for soliciting should be abolished. Indeed, it is not implausible to think of decriminalising it altogether, which perhaps makes as much sense, if not more, than the currently fashionable demand in the name of sexual equality to criminalise male kerb-crawlers as well.

Thus far we have argued that prison should not be used for the mentally ill, the habitual drunk, the maintenance defaulter, the prostitute and a whole range of petty persistent offenders. There are alternative sentences available and in most cases we have pointed to what these might involve. It is accepted that this leaves something to trust. To be fully convincing we would have to provide a much more exhaustive analysis of the alternatives on offer, though we have referred to some of them in more detail in earlier chapters, and organisations like NACRO have canvassed them relentlessly for more than a decade. Of course, it is important not to expect too much from these alternatives. They may well turn out to be no more successful in 'correcting' the offender's behaviour than prison. But to object to them on this basis is to miss the point, which is that while some offenders may well be trapped in a vicious cycle of social deprivation, even personal inadequacy, from which it is difficult to escape, this is hardly a reason for continuing to put them in prison.

Equally unjust can be the growing use of remand, particularly when it is imposed by magistrates for the wholly illegal purpose of giving offenders 'a taste of prison'. Since 1945, with the single exception of the detention centre population, the rate of increase in remand prisons has outstripped all other groups of prisoners. This has happened in spite of the Bail Act 1976 which created a statutory presumption in favour of bail. Conditions for prisoners on remand have become so bad as to be described as scandalous in the May Report. Prisoners are locked in their cells nearly all day and have few recreational facilities. In many ways their conditions are worse than those of convicted prisoners. This seems particularly unfair since something like 40 per cent of all remand prisoners are eventually judged to be either innocent or are given a non-custodial sentence. This fact alone indicates that many more remand prisoners could be safely released on bail than at present. Part of the problem stems from the fact that the police normally oppose bail if the defendent is homeless, a 'drifter' who is unlikely to turn up in court at a later date when his case is due to be heard again. There are several ways in which this difficulty might be overcome. To start with, the number of bail hostels should be increased. True, they are not always cheap to run, and in any case could never hope to offer places to everyone in need. However, the need might not be as great as some think. Homeless people are not always rootless, they often have strong ties with the local community and so are unlikely to abscond. A serious attempt to assess these ties should be made, perhaps even to the extent of helping defendants find temporary accommodation with friends – all this could help to lessen the need for prison.

Another vital consideration is the availability of legal advice. Very often defendants do not know how best to counter police objections to bail. Solicitors, on the other hand, should know exactly what is involved and can frequently negotiate informally with the police beforehand about what sort of conditions would be acceptable. The Law Society's recommendation for a 'duty solicitor' scheme to represent those defendants who would otherwise not have the benefit of legal advice when applying for bail is therefore to be welcomed. Not so acceptable is the Government's current proposal (1982) to enable remand hearings to take place in the defendant's absence. As things stand every remand prisoner has to appear in the magistrates' court every eight days. Under the new proposal, as long as a remand prisoner is legally represented and agrees, neither he nor his solicitor need appear. This might save the prison service and the courts both time and money, but it is likely to reduce the contact between remand prisoners and their solicitors, and the safeguard whereby the public can be satisfied that every remand prisoner is physically fit while at the same time, crucially, it is also likely to lead to less pressure on the courts to grant bail. The time spent by prisoners on remand is already far too long and the new proposal could well extend it. In 1978 the average waiting time between committal and trial was 9.6 weeks for those in custody. For some prisoners the delay is far longer. At one point in July 1977, for example, nearly 600 prisoners on remand had been waiting for trial or sentence for over three months. With remand periods generally lengthening there is a good case for introducing the Scottish system which ensures that once a person has been committed for trial then he or she must be brought before the courts and their trial concluded within 110 days.

To reduce the number of prisoners on remand, to develop non-custodial alternatives for petty offenders, the mentally ill, the habitually drunk and so on, all these measures would help to reduce the prison population and enable many offenders to avoid the futility of incarceration. Exactly how many would benefit is difficult to estimate, but in percentage terms it is very unlikely to exceed a quarter of the total prison population. This would still leave a lot of people on the inside, and if they are to be helped then other measures will have to be introduced.

Most obviously, perhaps, there must be changes in sentencing policy. Long prison sentences are popular with the English judiciary. Apart from satisfying some exaggerated desire for retribution this fact is difficult to understand since there is no evidence that long rather than short prison sentences have a beneficial effect on offenders. It was this that led the Advisory Council on the Penal System in its Interim Report on *The Length of Prison Sentences* to observe in 1977 that:

In many cases where there is a real choice available to the courts between a longer sentence and a shorter one . . . the court should bear in mind its general experience and the scientific evidence . . . and consider whether the balance should not be tipped in favour of a shorter sentence . . . The question we have to ask, in the light of all the evidence cited, is whether in this country we should maintain the level of sentencing which has become customary and indeed whether it is necessary to do so in order to prevent or reduce crime. (Paras 45 and 48.)

The short answer to this last question is that what we do in the penal system has little impact on the crime rate, which can only be explained in wider social terms; the crime rate is only marginally affected, if at all, by the punishments we hand out, their severity or frequency. This knowledge, plus the evidence that long sentences do little to benefit offenders, points towards the need for a substantial reduction in the length of prison sentences for just about all crimes, from housebreaking to very serious crimes involving assaults and armed robbery. Successive governments, it can reasonably be argued, have been aware of this need for some time now, and although they have not sought to legislate to reduce the length of prison sentences legally admissible, they have at least tried to influence the judiciary in a downward direction. At the highest levels this exhortation has had some impact. So, for example, the Court of Appeal has recently reduced the length of prison sentences imposed by lower courts and delivered quite detailed judgments clearly aimed at either keeping offenders out of prison altogether or reducing the length of time they spend there. This is commendable, but it is difficult not to agree with the House of Commons Home Affairs Committee that it is far short of what is really required. Exhortation, however well intended, will never bring about the changes in sentencing policy on the scale which is now required. What is clearly needed to reduce sentence lengths is legislation – the whole tariff system needs to be overhauled. There is no justification *whatsoever* for Conservative Home Secretary William Whitelaw's thinly veiled criticism that such a move would interfere with the traditional independence of the judiciary. Such a view is constitutional nonsense. For politicians to interfere directly in individual sentences might well be wrong, but it is Parliament's place to legislate on the level of legally permissible penalties and it is a political responsibility which all parties have to accept.

The public, it is true, may not respond to such a legislative initiative with much enthusiasm. After all, most people have been brought up on the idea that those who are sentenced to prison must be 'really dangerous' and therefore any move to cut their sentences is surely asking for trouble. But is it? The truth is that most offenders, and we are not now talking about petty persistent offenders or the habitually drunk, are not dangerous in the sense that most people take them to be, the sort of people who like ripping into the social fabric at every turn. Most could be given far shorter sentences without endangering the public and this would contribute substantially to a reduction in the overall level of the prison population. The Dutch experience is important here. True, the Netherlands has only a population of just over one-quarter of that of England and Wales, but it does show many of the same densely urban characteristics and it has had almost identical increases in reported crime to comparable proportionate levels. Yet its prison population is twelve times lower. This difference is partly explained by the way offenders are 'processed' through the Dutch legal system, which is very different from our own, but it also has something to do with the Dutch commitment to shorter sentences; at present 57 per cent of Dutch prisoners are serving sentences of under one month, while the average sentence is about two-and-a-half months. While not wishing to argue that the Dutch experience could necessarily be duplicated here, it does at least illustrate that shorter sentences can be imposed without any widespread danger to the public. It also shows what progress can be made without resorting to a whole plethora of alternative sentences such as Community Service Orders. The Dutch, it seems, have developed few alternatives to custody, a reluctance to prosecute unless really necessary, and short sentences as the main instruments of policy.

Some reduction in the present level of the prison population will probably be achieved by extending parole to include more short-term prisoners, as the Government intends. More effective though, would be to extend early release. There seemed a very real chance that this would happen in 1981. In that year an official *Review of Parole* suggested that prisoners serving over six months but less than three years should be entitled to early release after just one-third of their sentence. Not surprisingly, there were to be strings attached. That is, if a prisoner re-offended in the second third of his sentence, then he could be recalled and made to serve out his full sentence, depending on the discretion of the court. For prisoners serving over three years the *Review* suggested that parole should continue much as it does now. Home Secretary Whitelaw was known to be sympathetic to these proposals, but judicial opposition and the rough reception he was given at the Conservative Party

Conference in October 1981 made him change direction and choose the partially suspended sentence instead (see Ch. 3). This is regrettable. Early release should be introduced, and along the lines suggested in the *Review*, though with two important qualifications or additions. First, if early release were introduced then judges might well be tempted to increase sentences to compensate for any increase in remission. This is, of course, possible and although there is no evidence that it happened in Northern Ireland, where a similar scheme has been in operation since 1976, any scheme for increasing remission should be accompanied by legislation to reduce sentence lengths, as a prudent safeguard. Another difficulty is that the *Review* proposed to continue with parole for those prisoners serving sentences of over three years. This is entirely unacceptable. The idea that it is possible to determine when a prisoner has 'reached his peak', when he has been rehabilitated and can therefore be safely returned to the community, is just as fallacious as it ever was. Parole should be abolished and early release given to those prisoners serving over three years as well – they too should be let out after serving one-third of their sentence, and on the same conditions. The guiding principle behind all sentences, short or long, should be the seriousness of the offence committed, however difficult that might be to decide, rather than some fantasy about how long rehabilitation might take or some quite unproven relationship between sentence lengths and general deterrence.

It has been estimated that even if the new proposals for early release were introduced only for those prisoners serving sentences of between six months and three years, the prison population would drop by something like 7,000. If, then, early release was coupled with a reduction in the overall length of prison sentences a significant reduction in the prison population could be achieved, a downward trend which could be reinforced by the wide use of some of the more imaginative alternatives to custody we have already discussed. Such a reduction, which would obviously benefit those already on the inside and those about to be 'processed', would also help counter the Prison Department's militant campaign to secure 'more and better' prisons. Department officials claim that their outdated buildings are overcrowded, insanitary and in many cases about to fall down, literally. These claims are in some cases true, but the immediate way forward is not to build 'more and better' prisons, but to make far more sensible use of those we already have. As King and Morgan demonstrate, the Prison Department is seriously at fault here, the victim of its own rehabilitative ideology.[2] Local

Victorian prisons are seriously overcrowded, to the point of riot, in order to take pressure off training prisons where something called 'rehabilitation' is taking place. It is about time the Department saw through its own propaganda and spread the cruel weight of growing prison numbers more evenly.

If incarceration is to be avoided where possible for adults, the same should also apply to children. Indeed, there is a good case for keeping children out of the mainstream of the criminal justice system altogether. At the risk of sounding like an old-fashioned paragraph from a 1960s White Paper, most children who break the law quickly mature into sensible young people and to have them before the courts is in most cases quite unnecessary. Indeed, what evidence there is suggests that to label children as criminals all too easily compounds their drift into delinquency. Better caution than prosecution, then, is the best policy and there is some evidence that this might be happening. There are difficulties, though, such as the tendency for some police forces to issue official cautions even where there is insufficient evidence to prosecute.

When children are found guilty of criminal offences every effort should be made to keep them out of detention centres, Community Homes or residential assessment facilities. Far greater use should be made of fostering as an alternative to a spell in any one of these institutions whose achievements, to say the least, are overwhelmingly modest if not destructive. The fine, too, could be used more frequently. Too often children, just because they are children, are incarcerated, say for successive minor thefts which in the case of an adult would only have been punished by a modest fine or perhaps even a few hours community service. To put the same thing another way, many children who are no danger to society or to themselves are being plunged into the deep end of the juvenile penal system for no good reason. Incarceration in some cases is almost the *first* rather than the last resort. There is plenty of evidence to suggest how widespread this practice is, and it is one of the most worrying aspects of juvenile justice, which may come as a surprise to those who believe our social workers are far too liberal.

ON THE INSIDE

It is important to remember that while a strategy of decarceration and/or diversion may succeed in keeping large numbers of people out of prison there will still be plenty of people on the inside, in the short term anyway. Every attempt to secure justice and make life more tolerable for these prisoners should be supported. How hard that struggle is likely to be can be guessed at from the Government's refusal to take any disciplinary action against those prison officers involved in the MUFTI squad attack at Wormwood Scrubs in August 1979. It is difficult to imagine a more serious indictment of our political and administrative system than this inaction – to call it a public scandal is to be guilty of understatement. The appointment of a new Inspector of Prisons directly responsible to the Home Secretary but independent of the prison service might help here, though the publication of his investigations into 'special' incidents has been hedged around by important qualifications. At least his appointment should spare officials the embarrassment they must have felt when it was realised that the person asked to investigate the Scrubs affair was none other than the South-East Director of Prisons whose office had already issued a letter congratulating the staff on their handling of the incident! It is to be hoped that recent changes in Standing Orders arising out of judgments given by the European Commission on Human Rights at Strasbourg should make it easier for prisoners to speak out about disturbances like the one at the Scrubs, though it is important to remember that the Prison Rules themselves are still very much intact and are likely to continue as a formidable barrier to genuinely open communication.

Greater openness might be achieved by linking Boards of Visitors to local authorities. The Home Office has opposed this on the grounds that as local authorities have no statutory responsibility for running prisons they should 'keep out'. This tidy argument is little more than a defence of the *status quo*, an unwillingness to allow democratically elected representatives and their officers to advise and report on what are, after all, public institutions. This administrative arrogance needs to be challenged and local authorities should work with Boards of Visitors to create a continuous public forum in which they and their officials, say those concerned with environmental health or education, can meet with prison staff to review and discuss standards and actual provision. This should not only press the Home Office into making life more tolerable for those who, for the time being anyway, remain incarcerated, it should also help to educate the public about the hopelessness which underpins the whole prison system. It is still far too easy for those who run the system, and that includes Boards of Visitors, to engage in a closed debate and while this continues, while the public is prevented from witnessing the bankruptcy of the entire enterprise, then things are unlikely to change. This is why opening up the system is a 'negative' reform. That is, it is not intended as a reform to make prisons 'really work' or, indeed, just to make life more tolerable for those still on the inside – it is really about undermining the prison system, about reducing public confidence in its practice and potential.

As to the question of justice more directly, there is a good case for divesting Boards of Visitors of their disciplinary functions. As we have already seen, they are part of the prison administration; prison staff are involved in their regular meetings. In these circumstances Boards are never likely to be totally objective in settling disputes between prisoners and prison staff, however hard they might try, and because of this their powers to adjudicate and discipline should be passed, perhaps as the NCCL suggests, to a panel of lay assessors meeting with a legally qualified chairman. Another area of blurred responsibility concerns the prison medical service. This is a difficult area, and the problems are real ones. The prison doctor, presumably like any other doctor, has a responsibility for the well-being of his patients, to recommend practices which are beneficial to his health. Yet such a doctor is presumably expected to engage in practices, say helping prisoners to get through solitary by agreeing to issue tranquillisers, which are surely beneficial to no one's health. This clash of responsibilities is genuinely difficult to resolve, and this is to say nothing about allegations that difficult prisoners are involuntarily drugged for control purposes, that is, for non-medical reasons. In a closed, totalitarian institution like a prison the pressure on medical staff to drift towards a control function must be enormous and some way must be found to end their isolation. A good start would be to incorporate the service into the NHS and to make it responsible to area health authorities rather than to the Home Office which so far has not shown itself capable of understanding the problem.

For the children who are incarcerated there should be an end to indeterminate sentences which allow local authorities to release offenders only when they think fit. The length of any sentence imposed should be fixed and, as in the case of adults, determined by the seriousness of the offence committed. Legal representation should be available to all parents and children in cases where a custodial sentence is involved.

Finally, a word about secure units. These units have been favoured in recent years as an acceptable alternative to custody for unruly young offenders. At present there are just under 500 of these units available and about 150 are still under construction.

They are expensive to build, the capital cost averaging out at about £26,000 per unit, while to keep a child in one of these units for a year can apparently cost anything between £14,100 and £33,800. Such costs are staggering and even more staggering is that there was, and still is, no firm evidence that they achieve much. Indeed, the only two available studies suggest that in some ways they might be doing more harm than good. Created as an act of political expediency, they should be abolished.

JUSTICE AND PROSPECTS

Although the alternative penal policy we have so far outlined is necessarily limited in detail, little more than a rough sketch, the principles behind it indicate clearly enough a sympathy towards what we referred to earlier as the justice model. This approach to the penal system is sometimes criticised by radicals on several grounds. In the first place, they argue that it is ludicrous to talk of a just penal system in an unequal society which is weighted against low income groups, blacks and other disadvantaged minorities; these are traditionally the groups who feel the weight of the penal system on their backs, the people who overflow from our insanitary prisons and Borstals. This evaluation is difficult to quarrel with; criminal acts are committed by all social classes yet it is predominantly those from the lower socio-economic classes who are brutalised by what we euphemistically call the correctional system. Who, then, can reasonably talk of justice? How has such an inappropriate model gained so much currency? For Marxists the explanation is associated with their belief that the search for alternatives to prison was not the result of some blinding liberal insight into the futility of incarceration but a practical policy response to the British state's galloping fiscal crisis. As they see it, the justice model is in effect and at a crucial ideological level, simply a reflection of this shift, a model which by taking as its rationale the 'now proven futility of incarceration' actually helps to obscure or hide the real material basis of the change in British penal policy. A change, by the way, which has been slow to come about because the very intensity of the State's present fiscal crisis has ruptured the consensus of the 1950s and 1960s, and the law-and-order authoritarian consensus which has been orchestrated to replace it cannot easily be seen to be 'going soft' on alternatives. Another way of exploring the same argument is to think of the 1960s and rehabilitation as a time when sufficient surpluses were being generated for the State to support the expensive ideology of institutional treatment, to go along with the idea that offenders are ill and in need of psychiatric help 'on the inside'. Now that these surpluses are no longer being generated it is easier to believe what has, in fact, always been known, that prisons do not work and in the present climate to see prisoners as rational, or feckless, and more in need of relatively cheap community-based *punishment* pure and simple, with no treatment strings attached.

In our view the fit of these arguments is by no means as neat as some radicals would like us to believe. Some alternatives, take Day Training Centres as an example, are arguably more expensive than incarceration. However, the main thrust of their argument has a lot to recommend it. As we pointed out earlier, prisons as we now understand them are very much the product of the Industrial Revolution. They represent a significant social investment. Large constructions like Pentonville, Wandsworth and Strangeways cost a lot to build, a fact which did not go unnoticed. There were also moves to institutionalise and segregate other 'marginal' groups. Workhouses for the unemployed in the years following the Poor Law Amendment Act 1834 are just one example. The capital required to make this investment was then being generated. Once this ceases to be so, when the State is confronted by a serious and prolonged fiscal crisis, then it seems reasonable to suppose that much of the institutional provision we take for granted will be scaled down and the services they provide offered, if at all, in an alternative and less costly form. Some would argue that this transition is well under way, as in the provision of community alternatives for the mentally ill.

This is to seriously overstate the case. If widespread decarceration, to stretch the term somewhat, is to come at all, then it will take a long time, and its progress between different sorts of institutions, and over time, is likely to be uneven, which in a general way might help to explain the obvious fact that its progress to date has been modest. After all, this is not the first fiscal crisis to affect the British State, far from it. There *are* other factors at work, clearly. However, what is important about this long progress towards decarceration is that in the intervening years there are still going to be plenty of people 'on the inside' and their interests have to be fought for, even if it means arguing for selected progressive demands which are now associated with the justice model; for example, the abolition of parole. The fact that those 'on the inside' are in many cases victims too, victims of an unequal society and a discriminatory system of criminal justice, in no way invalidates such a strategy. To say otherwise is surely to counsel despair, to believe that nothing can be done in the face of oppression. It is not unlike the sort of simple view RAP used to hold about the criminal law, namely, that it operates in the interests of the ruling class. Indeed it might, and very often does, but it can also be used as a vehicle to defend working-class interests. It is not unlike the State, a 'space' to be contended for. To say otherwise is to engage in a sort of crude reductionism which does not allow sufficient flexibility to explain why, to give just one example, the judiciary can and do make judgments which are against the interests of capital.

We began by arguing that imprisonment was a brutalising experience, that in the short term as many offenders as possible should be handled in other ways. We have ended by referring to the 'long progress towards decarceration'. This indicates not only that we see a progression, it also implies that perhaps abolition, through a series of negative or undermining reforms, is the final goal, as indeed it is. The idea of prison abolition raises a number of serious questions. To take first what Stan Cohen has called graphically the 'Jack the Ripper' question.[3] This is often raised by people who are by no means unsympathetic to the idea of closing our prisons, who realise well enough that most offenders could be safely handled in the community. What worries them are the few, the 'really dangerous' offenders. Can they too be reasonably handled within the community? The honest answer must be no, and so for some offenders at least, perhaps under 10 per cent, some time spent in custody seems inevitable. But exactly who are these 'really dangerous' offenders, how do we recognise and sentence them? According to the nature of their offence? Or on the basis of some prediction about their future behaviour? Faced with these choices it is difficult not to agree with Cohen and others that offenders should be punished on the basis of their offence, on what they have done rather than what they might do. There simply is no reliable way of predicting an offender's future behaviour and so to sentence on such a basis could (and does) lead to serious injustices, of offenders being held in custody for far longer periods than is really necessary.[4]

The prospect for abolition also runs into other difficulties, particularly from radicals. To start with, if the criminal justice system does discriminate against the poor, the weak and the disadvantaged, surely prison abolition will do nothing to alter this, the same people will end up being 'processed' and labelled. And what is more, argue some radicals, many of the alternatives to prison now on offer are themselves fairly coercive, in danger of becoming 'prisons without walls'. In these circumstances it might be 'better' to put up with prisons – they are at least far less oblique and stand out as 'stark symbols of basic social control and repression' in an unequal class-divided society. Such a conclusion must be wrong. What this line of argument surely suggests is not an acceptance of 'things as they are' but the need to develop criteria which (a) discriminate between those alternatives already on offer – some must be better than others, and (b) which can act as organising principles for developing other and more genuinely radical alternatives which help those who are oppressed to 'survive' and, perhaps, even fight back. With a few notable exceptions there has been little attempt to think this sort of strategy through, and much the same could be said about devising ways to combat the newly-constructed and authoritarian law-and-order consensus. True, groups like Class and Justice have made a contribution here, stressing the need for more effective democratic control of the police, and this has been taken up by the Labour Party whose search for a 'framework' within which to discuss law and order might do far worse than to start with Ian Taylor's recently published *Law and Order: Arguments for Socialism* (1981), before getting tied down by Roy Hattersley's tough-minded pragmatism.[5]

More conventionally, perhaps, all this emphasis on offenders is likely to provoke a sharp response from many people who will demand, 'But what about the victim?' This concern is not misplaced. Far too much money and effort goes into combating crime and condemning the criminal; it would be far more sensible to redirect some of these resources to help victims. In cash terms, an immediate start could be made by cutting the police force substantially and using the money saved to establish a property compensation fund which would be used to reimburse victims for property losses up to a fixed amount. It is no excuse for the Government to reject such a scheme on the grounds that most people now insure their property. What about those, say the old, the sick and the poor, who cannot afford to insure their often modest possessions; are they to be ignored? The scope of the Criminal Injuries Compensation Board could also be extended. Set up in 1964, the Board paid out over £13,000,000 in the financial year 1978/79. The Board can now, sensibly, make compensation awards to those victims who have suffered from violence within the family (since 1979). There is no good reason, though, why the lower limit on claims should stand as high as £150, and this should be reduced. Of course what victims usually want, in the short term anyway, is not so much financial help as neighbourly aid and comfort. To provide this a number of voluntary victim-support schemes have been established and these should be encouraged. Financial support should also be given to rape crisis centres and more refuges set up for battered wives. Practical help for victims *is* important.

Finally, although abolition may well be a long-term goal, many of our short-term proposals, if introduced, would make a significant contribution to reducing the present level of the prison population. As a first step towards ending the prolonged crisis in our penal system this reduction is essential. What is depressing, though, is the knowledge that many of our proposals are by no means new or revolutionary, indeed they are fairly obvious. Many groups have put forward similar packages, including groups like NACRO which is close to government to say the least. No one wants to imprison drunks or the mentally ill or even keep 'average' offenders on the inside for any longer than is necessary, yet the prison population continues to rise and the Criminal Justice Bill 1981 now before Parliament seems unlikely to *significantly* reduce this trend – that at least is the view of the lobby. True, the Bill so far amended does include some gains. Vagrants and prostitutes, for example, should no longer face the immediate threat of imprisonment. The power enabling magistrates to commit young offenders to secure care has also been 'watered down'. Balanced against these modest gains, however, is the real threat posed by the provision for shorter minimum detention centre orders which many people fear could conceivably sharply increase the number of young offenders held in custody.

How is all this to be explained, particularly the past ten years, the continuous pressure on the penal system and, in particular, on prisons? It is tempting to look at the policy process and to blame an incompetent and secret civil service. It is no less tempting to single out for blame a hard-nosed judiciary and, of course, civil servants and ignorant judges must take their share of the blame. However, it is difficult not to see the present crisis in the penal system in far wider and more obviously political terms. For those people who are anxious about such an approach, this does not necessarily involve a radical commitment, least of all to some all-embracing single theory. On the other hand, it would be plain pig-headed not to accept that our society is now more bitterly divided than at any time since the Second World War and that those divisions have been policed in an increasingly authoritarian way under the banner of 'law and order'. It is this wider political crisis which has put pressure on the penal system, which generated the imperative that this was 'no time to be going soft', to introduce what were seen as liberalising measures. Until this crisis is resolved any significant change in the direction of penal policy seems unlikely. The recent suggestion that a 'curfew' should be imposed on young offenders whose disregard for the law is apparently to be traced back to what Mrs Thatcher calls the 'permissive claptrap of the 1960s', shows just how well entrenched the crisis has become.

REFERENCES

1. Cmnd 3909, *Report on the Enforcement of Judgement Debts* (HMSO: London, 1969) para 1099.
2. R. KING and D. MORGAN, *Crisis in the Prisons* (University of Bath: 1979).
3. S. COHEN, *Crime and Punishment* (RAP: London, 1979).
4. For the sort of régime which might be tried for 'really dangerous' offenders there is Scotland's example, the Special Unit at Barlinnie prison which housed Jimmy Boyle.
5. For Hattersley on the police and other law and order issues see *New Socialist* No. 6, (July/Aug. 1982).

SELECT BIBLIOGRAPHY

L. BLOM-COOPER, *The A6 Murder* (Penguin: Harmondsworth, 1963).

A. E. BOTTOMS and R. H. PRESTON (eds), *The Coming Penal Crisis* (Scottish Academic Press: Edinburgh, 1980).

J. BOYLE, *A Sense of Freedom* (Pan: London, 1977).

J. B. CHRISTOPH, *Capital Punishment and British Politics* (Allen & Unwin: London, 1962).

S. COHEN, *Crime and Punishment* (RAP: London, 1979).

S. COHEN and L. TAYLOR, *Psychological Survival*, (Penguin: Harmondsworth, 1972).

S. COHEN and L. TAYLOR, *Prison Secrets* (NCCL and RAP: London, 1978).

T. P. COOGAN, *On the Blanket* (Ward River Press: Dublin, 1980).

D. DOWNES and P. ROCK, *Deviant Interpretations* (Martin Robertson: London, 1979).

R. FINE *et al.*, *Capitalism and the Rule of Law* (Hutchinson: London, 1979).

M. FITZGERALD, *Prisoners in Revolt* (Penguin: Harmondsworth, 1977).

M. FOUCAULT, *Discipline and Punish* (Allen Lane: London, 1977).

S. HALL *et al.*, *Policing the Crisis* (Macmillan: London, 1978).

J. E. HALL-WILLIAMS, *The English Penal System in Transition* (Butterworth & Co.: London, 1970).

D. HAXBY, *Probation: A Changing Service* (Constable: London, 1978).

R. HOOD (ed.), *Crime, Criminology and Public Policy* (Heinemann: London, 1974).

M. IGNATIEFF, *A Just Measure of Pain* (Macmillan: London, 1978).

T. MATHIESEN, *The Politics of Abolition* (Martin Robertson: London, 1974).

D. MATZA, *Becoming Deviant* (Prentice Hall: New Jersey, 1969).

J. McVICAR, *McVicar by Himself* (Arrow: London, 1979).

R. MORGAN, *Formulating Penal Policy* (NACRO: London, 1979).

National Deviancy Conference, *Permissiveness and Social Control* (Macmillan: London, 1980)

N. NUGENT and R. KING (eds), *Respectable Rebels* (Hodder & Stoughton: London, 1979).

F. PEARCE, *Crimes of the Powerful* (Pluto Press: London, 1976).

PRISON RESEARCH EDUCATION ACTION PROJECT, *Instead of Prisons* (PREAP: Syracuse, New York, 1976).

PRISONERS AID COMMITTEE, *Irish Voices from English Jails* (Prisoners Aid Committee: London, 1979).

R. QUINNEY, *Class, State and Crime* (Longman: New York, 1977).

L. RADZINOWICZ and J. KING, *The Growth of Crime* (Penguin: Harmondsworth, 1977).

P. ROCK and M. McINTOSH, *Deviance and Social Control* (Tavistock: London, 1974).

G. ROSE, *The Struggle for Penal Reform* (Stevens: London, 1961).

M. RYAN, *The Acceptable Pressure Group: A case-study of the Howard League and RAP* (Gower: Farnborough, 1978).

A. SCULL, *Decarceration* (Prentice Hall: New Jersey, 1977).

C. SMART, *Women, Crime and Criminology* (Routledge & Kegan Paul: London, 1976).

I. TAYLOR, *Law and Order: Arguments for Socialism* (Macmillan: London, 1981).

I. TAYLOR, P. WALTON and J. YOUNG, *Critical Criminology* (Routledge & Kegan Paul: London, 1975).

I. TAYLOR, P. WALTON and J. YOUNG, *The New Criminology* (Routledge & Kegan Paul: London, 1973)

J. E. THOMAS, *The English Prison Officer Since 1850* (Routledge & Kegan Paul: London, 1972).

N. WALKER (ed.), *Penal Policy-making in England* (Cambridge Institute of Criminology: Cambridge, 1977).

P. WILES, *Crime and Delinquency in Britain*, Vol. II (Martin Robertson: London, 1976).

B. WOOTTON, *Crime and Penal Policy* (Allen & Unwin: London, 1978).

INDEX

abortion, 27, 32, 46
Adult Offender (1965), 34, 37
Advisory Council on the Penal System (ACPS), 34, 49, 50, 53, 65, 67, 73, 76, 77, 78, 79, 80, 88, 93, 129
Advisory Council on the Treatment of Offenders (ACTO), 28, 29, 73, 75, 76, 106
Ali, Tariq, 98
Alternative Economic Strategy, 46
alternatives to custody, 49–53, 72, 103, 131, 132
alternatives to prison, 4, 67, 70, 72, 107, 111, 120, 125–9, 138
alternative society, 98
Amnesty, 58
Angry Brigade, 57–8
anti-Vietnam War campaign, 98
Approved Schools, 19, 20, 28, 31, 33, 55
attendance centres, 28, 31
Avebury, Lord, 70

Bail Act (1976), 65, 128
Behan, B., 19
Benson, G., 19, 20, 106
Bentham, J., 2, 25
Bentley, D., 14, 16, 39
Bevan, A., 14
Biggs, R., 35
Birmingham Evening Mail, 118
Black Act, 3
Blake, G., 35, 42
Boards of Visitors, 58, 63, 64, 83, 134–5

Borstal, 2, 33, 50, 53, 108
    overcrowding 17, 22, 33
    population, 17, 19, 55; black, 114
    regime 53
    system 8, 9, 17, 20, 23, 87
    training 9, 17, 23, 28
    sentences 53, 54, 56
Bottoms, A. E., 69
Boyson, R., 32, 54, 101
Braddock, B., 19
Brady, I., 41
Brayshaw, A. J., 67
British Association of Social Workers, 115
Brittan, L., 67
Brockway, Lord, 58
Brooke, H., 75
Butler, R. A., 24, 25, 27, 74, 78, 80, 96, 97, 99, 100

Callaghan, J., 37, 39, 41
Calvert, R., 10
Cambridge Institute of Criminology, 74, 75, 99, 111
capital punishment, 10–16, 22, 27, 39–42, 46, 61–2, 68, 88, 96, 99
Care Order 31, 54
Carlisle, M., 109
Carlton House, 20, 28
Carr, R., 48, 58
certificates of unruliness, 56, 94
Chapell, P., 115
Child, The Family and the Young Offender (1965), 29, 30, 34
Children and Young Persons Act (1969), 31, 44, 54–7, 91, 115, 118